KINGDOM MINDED

Learning to Walk in Discipline as a Follower of Christ

MARY GAUTREAUX

KINGDOM MINDED
Learning to Walk in Discipline as a Follower of Christ

By Mary C. Gautreaux

Copyright © July 2019
Wisdom House Publishing
2003 Stapleton Dr., Friendswood, TX 77546

www.WisdomHousePubs.com
281.352.6540

All rights reserved. No part of this book may be reproduced, stored in a retrieval system or transmitted, in any form or by any means, electronic, photocopying, recording, or otherwise, without written permission of the publisher.

Unless otherwise noted, all Scripture references are from the Holy Bible, New International Version®, NIV® Copyright © 1973, 1978, 1984, 2011 by Biblica, Inc.® Used by permission. of Zondervan. All rights reserved worldwide. www.zondervan.com.

Cover design: Jay Loucks, John Magee
ISBN: 978-0-578-53045-1
Printed in the United States of America

Dedicated to my parents,
Charles and Judy.
Thank you for life, laughter, love and wings.

Contents

Preface		7
1.	An Introduction to Discipline	11
2.	Two Kingdoms	17
3.	What It Takes	23
4.	What Stands in the Way	29
5.	Surrender	37
6.	Can it Really be that Simple?	43
7.	Self-Control	51
8.	Building Blocks for a Healthy Spiritual Life	61
9.	Bringing Order to Disorder in Mind, Body and Spirit	71
10.	A Life That Matters	83
11.	A City on a Hill	91
12.	There is More	99
13.	The Discipline of Waiting	107
14.	Changed	113
References		119

Preface

For you were once darkness, but now you are light in the Lord. Live as children of light (for the fruit of the light consists in all goodness, righteousness and truth) and find out what pleases the Lord. Have nothing to do with the fruitless deeds of darkness, but rather expose them. It is shameful even to mention what the disobedient do in secret. But everything exposed by the light becomes visible—and everything that is illuminated becomes a light. This is why it is said: "Wake up, sleeper, rise from the dead, and Christ will shine on you." Ephesians 5: 8-14

My husband and I have spent the last twenty-seven years as campus pastors with Chi Alpha Campus Ministries at Sam Houston State University. We have two wonderful daughters, one terrific son-in-law, a beautiful new grandson, and an incredibly supportive and loving extended family, both biologically and spiritually. I am an ordained minister with the Assemblies of God with an undergraduate degree in Elementary Education. I taught school for a few years just out of college and began work on a Master's degree in English as a Second Language, but then gladly put the brakes on that with the arrival of our first daughter. Perhaps I will resume official studies eventually, but in the meantime, I have kept busy raising and homeschooling our kids, playing an active role in the student ministry, and reading and studying as much as I can on my own.

My husband and I recently transitioned to a new position, as district overseers for Chi Alpha throughout much of Texas, so now seemed like a great time and opportunity to share a few things we have learned along the way.

Eli and I both began walking with Jesus as college students in 1990. We have extensive experience in learning to walk in spiritual discipline. We have also had the privilege of watching thousands of others begin on their own journey with the Lord. We firmly believe in deliberate discipleship for all Christians, especially for new believers.

It is vital for young believers to learn how to walk with God, so we can become strong and effective Christians who make a difference in this hurting world. It makes me think of a friend who recently gave birth. It would be tragic, after the miracle of childbirth, for her and her husband to leave their vulnerable infant to raise herself, saying, "Good luck, little one! We are so glad you were born! See you when we all get to heaven!" We cannot do that to new Christians, either! After the miracle of a new birth, mature believers must take the time to care for and to help young believers learn to grow in the grace and knowledge of God. Discipleship matters.

This book deals with the idea of discipline as Christians: what it means, how we practice it, why it is important, and why it is so difficult. The first four chapters lay out a map for understanding our need for spiritual discipline, and the remainder of the chapters explore the development of a "kingdom" mindset. I must confess that I have frequently written about this subject over the years, primarily because I recognize I need much more of it in my own life. My husband is incredibly disciplined, and his life and good practices have always challenged me to grow in this area. Please consider these chapters as coaching sessions to myself that I love sharing with you!

Most of all, I want to encourage you. Whether you have been a Christian for a month, a decade or a lifetime, the best is truly yet to come. You may have fallen down, or missed an opportunity; you might even find yourself currently stuck in a terrible rut, but the race is not over yet. God's mercies are new every single day,

PREFACE

and today is a great day to begin a fresh start.

—Huntsville, Texas
March 2019

ONE

An Introduction to Discipline

Every good and perfect gift is from above, coming down from the Father of the heavenly lights, who does not change like shifting shadows. James 1:17

When I was young, my family lived in New England. My father was in the Navy, so although we are a family with deep Texas roots, we spent a great deal of my childhood in Connecticut. It is such an incredibly beautiful part of the country, rich with history which you can see and experience daily. In the woods right behind our home were remnants of stone fences that someone, hundreds of years earlier, built as they were settling the land. Most towns have that quintessential New England look about them, with the quaint, wooden church standing proudly in the town center and the rest of the village built up around it. The elements of orderliness and practicality still remain in the towns that the earliest Europeans settled as they came to this side of the world, and this just adds to the beauty and charm of New England.

Most summers, we would travel with family and friends to a place called Tanglewood, which is an outdoor theater in Massachusetts, where we would listen to the Boston Symphony Orchestra perform. After beginning the day with a grand picnic spread, the remainder of the day was spent lounging in the cool green grass under the shade trees, enjoying the glorious music, good company, and more food. My childhood was pretty idyllic, and this summertime experience is a highlighted memory for me—especially the time that the featured music was *The Four Seasons* by Antonio Vivaldi. Somehow all of that wonderful experience is wrapped together in my mind, and to this day, when I hear that lovely music, all of those good feelings come along with it.

Celebrating and looking forward to each of the four seasons has always been a special joy for me. Growing up in the northeast, I experienced the real and welcome change from spring, to the lazy warm-sunshine months of summer, to the crisp and brilliant months of autumn, to the long, snow-cold winter, and back again to the sunshine and flowers of spring. In Texas, our four seasons are not as sharply distinct, but they are still highly anticipated changes every year, as each season brings with it something new and refreshing.

This world is an incredible picture and testimony of the nature and character of God! Think about how He made the world. I love to read and re-read the Genesis account of the beginning of this beautiful world we live in, a world full of wonder and, yes, discipline. Think what Scripture says. The light and darkness have boundaries, as do the oceans and land. There are four distinct seasons that obediently follow one another. The yearly life cycle of trees and flowers, animals and their young, rains, snows, dryness, seed time, and harvest—the entire earth operates within its God-given boundaries of orderliness and discipline. The earth revolves around the sun, which gives just the right amount of light and darkness to keep everything moving and growing and healthy. Everything is dependent upon God and the boundaries which He has ordained.

Think about how He made human beings this way, as well. He made us, male and female, in an incredible array of skin colors

AN INTRODUCTION TO DISCIPLINE

and personalities, each reflecting unique characteristics of His own image. He instituted the wondrous miracle of reproduction, our bodies forming and growing in our mothers' wombs until birth. Then with this glorious miracle of life, we all grow and learn and develop at a perfect rate, with built-in rhythms of wakefulness and sleep, eating and drinking to replenish what energy we expend, and cells that know how to recharge properly each day. We are infants, then children, and eventually adults who marry and start the cycle all over again, caring for and training the next generation, until finally we are elderly and they care for us. These are the rhythms and seasons to life that God made for us. They are consistent and they are good.

Now think about God Himself—perfect, unchanging, faithful, steadfast; "the same yesterday, today and forever" (Heb. 13:8). Like the passage in the Epistle of James says, He does not change like shifting shadows (James 1:17). It is interesting to note here that James grew up with Jesus, who was his older half-brother. He could write with all truth that God does not change: James lived with Jesus, the Son of God, the exact representation of God. James would have seen firsthand Jesus' amazing, unchanging character. God is always caring, always faithful, always unselfishly choosing for the highest good. He exists in true freedom, and from this everything else in the universe flows. His character creates the healthy boundary of the universe, marking out the way we should grow and act and live.

God does not have bad moods. He never says anything He wishes He could take back. Everything He does, has ever done, or ever will do, is perfect and in order. The fruit of His Spirit (read Gal. 5) define His character. That is to say, God does not just exhibit love, joy, peace, patience, kindness, goodness, gentleness, faithfulness and self-control—He actually is love, and He is peace, and He is joy. All the fruit of the Spirit we can read about in Galatians are descriptors of the nature and character of God, including self-control. God is self-control; He is discipline.

This brings us to our subject. Discipline is a word which rubs many people the wrong way. We equate discipline only with being in trouble. Or, if we are honest with ourselves, we bristle at the thought of anyone stepping in and telling us what to do. Discipline flies directly in the face of our fallen, sinful nature's mantra, "Don't tell me what to do." Yes, discipline involves correction and redirection, but it is so much more than that.

Let me define discipline as restoring order from disorder in the mind, body and spirit. For example, try to remember your childhood home and your often messy room, or perhaps a dorm room in college. Imagine you have gone for days or even weeks without putting anything away, just tossing books, clothes and everything else somewhere as you fall into bed for the night. Day by day the disorder increases until you can barely function. You do not have any clean clothes left, and you could not possibly find them even if you did! Eventually you have to spend an entire day cleaning, organizing and putting things away—restoring order to disorder. Can you remember how good it felt when you were finished?

This is a great place to begin the study of spiritual discipline as a Christian. Discipline is restoring order to disorder in the mind, body and spirit of a follower of Jesus. Discipline is the means to bringing and maintaining godly order in our lives. We must realize that true freedom is not the lack of boundaries. Real freedom comes from consistently living within safe and healthy boundaries. Think how chaotic life would be if God Himself was suddenly unsteady and moody! Everything in the universe would fall apart. Now, think about how much less chaotic our own lives would be if we simply stayed in bounds, if we walked in consistent discipline like God.

Discipline is the path we follow as disciples (see the similarity of those words?), as we move into a deeper knowledge of God, keep in step with the Holy Spirit, and are conformed into the image of Jesus. God is discipline, and there has never been a day since time without beginning that He was unsteady or chose the wrong path. He made us in His image, which means we can learn and grow and become more like Him every day. We can become steady and faithful. The disciplined ordering of our lives here and now, bringing beauty from chaos, will help us live more effectively now and get us more and more ready to be citizens of heaven forever.

Application

When we read something about God or that is devotional in nature, it is a great habit to immediately apply what we have read to our lives. A fitting step after this chapter would be to pray and know God hears and helps us when we cry out to Him:

God, I thank You that You are so good and You are so faithful. I am grateful that You do not leave us alone. You have made each of us in Your image and You help us to become more like Yourself all the time. I ask that You would help me learn and grow. Please help me apply order and discipline to my life, so that I can become a steady man or woman of God. I love You and thank You for all that You do. In Jesus' name, amen.

TWO

Two Kingdoms

When a person becomes a Christian, accepting Jesus as Lord and Savior of his life, many incredible and intense changes happen. In John 3, we read that Jesus considered the change to be so great He called it being "born again." At the point of salvation, we all begin a great journey. There are some huge theological pieces to this, but for our discussion we can make it simple.

Imagine that you were born and raised in a tiny village on the most remote mountain somewhere on the other side of the world. You grew up in a certain way and were accustomed to speaking, eating, dressing and living life in a particular manner. There was no electricity or access to the outside world, and each day was simply based around survival—making sure everyone in the village had enough to eat and was well protected from the elements and wild animals. Now imagine that one night you go to sleep, but wake up the next morning in a high-rise apartment in the middle of Manhattan. You are still wearing your usual garments and you are still thinking in your native language, but nothing around you

KINGDOM MINDED

is familiar at all—not the room, the food, the street signs or the sounds; nothing. You have to learn to navigate life in this new world, which is almost overwhelming at first, but also exciting and full of wonders.

This is similar to what a person experiences spiritually when he or she is born again. We grew up entirely immersed in another way of life, so much so that we did not know there was any other way to live. There was a certain way of thinking, speaking and acting that was normal to us, and there were customs and traditions that were so familiar they felt normalized.

The "new normal" we experience as we give our lives to Jesus and begin walking with Him is often such a surprise. For example, my mother-in-law told me that when she accepted Christ at the age of forty-three, she kept looking into mirrors to see if she was really smiling because for the first time in her life, she felt she was smiling all the time. When she met Jesus, He lifted a bitterness and heaviness of heart that she had carried for decades, and she could feel the difference in her spirit. What is this abrupt and massive change?

The story of this age we live in is a tale of two very real, spiritual kingdoms. One is a realm that everyone can see and which we are all born into: the kingdom of darkness. It covers the whole earth and is the rotten source of all of the evil, injustice and wickedness in the world. This kingdom was born out of supreme selfishness. It came into being when one willful creature said to God, "I know better." From that point on, darkness entered God's beautiful creation; this is sin which is separation from God. That dark one managed to convince others to follow him in rebellion, and staged the greatest treachery against God when it convinced His perfect and favored creation, man and woman, to eat of the tree of the knowledge of good and evil (Gen. 2:17) so they could be like God" and join in the rebellious shout of, "I know better!"

This kingdom of darkness is fueled by selfishness. In fact, the two prevailing attitudes of this kingdom are "Me first," and, "I am better than you." Everyone is living for himself, and it does not matter how many others have to be climbed on or pushed out of the way. The currencies of this kingdom are money and power, and the result of loyalty to this kingdom is death—separation from God forever. The devil is the prince of this realm, and he hates God so much that he does everything he can to make the creation of God fruitless and despairing. He is the Prince of Darkness, but he has already been defeated by Jesus and His great work on the cross. He knows his time is short, and will do all that he can to kill, steal and destroy men and women, boys and girls, and keep them in His kingdom forever. He wants everyone to stay blind to spiritual realities or to give themselves to the gods of darkness—anything but know the true God.

In the kingdom of darkness, the motive is selfishness and the end is destruction, so the more selfish and sensual an activity is, the better. This kingdom says if anything feels good, do it, and if you feel inclined to do something, act on it immediately regardless of the cost to yourself or others. It makes this prince rejoice when people are confused, anxious, depressed, drunk, high, suicidal, murderous and rapacious. The more people he can kill, the more satisfied he is because he has caused pain to God. The more good things he can take away from his subjects, the better. The values of this kingdom are clearly reflected in the favorite pastimes of its citizens, so its songs celebrate lust, greed, destruction and despair. It is no surprise that so many citizens of this kingdom try to stay numb somehow in order to survive in such a place.

On the glorious other hand, there is the kingdom of light. This is the eternal kingdom, the one that has existed from time without beginning, and which will continue forever. This is the kingdom of God, the creator of the universe and King of all kings. The prevailing attitude of His kingdom is true love and thorough unselfishness: others first, others matter, others are also loved by the King and made in His image. It is a place of informed, consistent, conscious choices, choices for the highest good of God and His kingdom[2].

The King is a Father who wants the best for all of His children, and is always actively at work for that end. He saw the invasion of darkness from its beginning, and had a masterful plan to counter the rebellion, one so audacious that darkness never suspected. This King gave His only Son as a ransom for the price of sin, so that everyone who accepts this gift of life can be born again, coming out of the darkness into the kingdom of light.

The work of this kingdom is for every child of the King to proclaim the Good News of salvation until Jesus returns to usher in a new age. Everywhere, all the time, the Good News is passed on, and others are born again into the kingdom of light. People are the currency of this kingdom; souls are of highest value. Citizens of this kingdom are filled with light, peace, life and joy, bringing them strength, regardless of circumstance. In fact, the great love of God causes His people from every walk of life, in every situation, to be able to walk in strength and dignity, full of security, confident and hopeful for the future. The songs of this kingdom radiate love, healing and hope, knowing this present world is not the end, but simply a stepping stone to forever in the presence of God and one another in His great city.

When you and I were born again, our hearts were opened to the kingdom of light for the first time. After years of trudging through the dark, we can now breathe the clean, free air of God's kingdom. Before, while swimming along in muddy, filthy water, we could not notice how polluted it was. Until our eyes were opened, we could not even see how fruitless and hopeless things were. When we accepted Jesus, we became destined for heaven, where we will be with God forever. This is great news!

There is one problem, however! Imagine that you are preparing to go on a lengthy road trip to a place you have always wanted to go. Can you imagine going on that trip with someone unpleasant? That would take the fun right out of what should be a terrific experience! In college, I once found myself driving across the entire breadth of the country with two people who did not care for deodorant or soap, and that was a long journey! Or have you ever had a difficult roommate; you know, the one who ate all your ice cream, or who never even washed one dish? It is frustrating to have to be with someone difficult or selfish or rude for any length of time. Are you seeing the problem yet?

Heaven is glorious and pure. It is lighted by the very presence of Holy God. If we arrive there in the condition we were the moment we were born again, heaven would immediately cease to be so heavenly. Now it is important to note that being "good enough" is in no way a prerequisite for salvation; none of us could ever be good enough. Salvation is a free, undeserved gift from God. Jesus Himself assured the dying thief on the cross that he would be with Him that very day in Paradise (Luke 23:43), and that man certainly did not have time to practice any disciplines or be conformed into the image of Christ. All he did, all any of us have to do, is believe and confess that Jesus is Lord.

But the Bible also teaches that we will someday be given positions of authority and leadership in heaven, and that now is the time to prepare for eternity. If we are responsible with what we are given here, we will be entrusted with much there (1 Cor. 6:2-3).

This brings us right back around to why discipline is so important for a Christian. We need to be ready for anything life throws our way here on earth, and we need to be ready to live forever in heaven. Once we are born again, we have to learn to walk with God, and we have to let Him conform us into His image. We have to get some practices and parameters in our lives that eradicate what we learned and lived in the kingdom of darkness, making us into productive citizens of the kingdom of light for all eternity. Today's discipline is shaping us for eternal duties.

Application

Read Colossians 3:5-17. This is a letter the Apostle Paul wrote to a group of believers, encouraging them to put away their earthly nature. In verses 5-11, he lists the things they did (and maybe still do) in their earthly nature, then in verses 12-17, he contrasts that with how God's people should live.

Where do you find yourself when you read this? Do not be discouraged by this in any way. We all have to start somewhere. Paul knew human nature as well as anyone, calling himself the "chief of sinners," referring to his persecutions of the Church, and participating in the murder of one of Jesus' disciples before he was a Christian (Acts 7)!

Be honest with yourself and God about where you are, and where you would like to be. Colossians 3:5 says, "Put to death, therefore, whatever belongs to your earthly nature." A great first step is to repent (stop and turn away from) of one of the things you do in your earthly nature. Take a moment to ask God to show you which one He would like you to deal with first. We know that God speaks to us through the Bible, and He also speaks to us in times of prayer. Listen, and you will find that He is speaking to you.

Now begin to make this a matter of prayer. Truly ask God to forgive you and change you. Ask Him to help you make a concrete plan to leave this sin behind. If you have a trusted friend or group of friends (and I hope you do), confess to them and let them help you walk away from your sinful nature. This is an important part of your journey to become more like Christ.

THREE

What It Takes

Do you not know that in a race all the runners run, but only one gets the prize? Run in such a way as to get the prize. Everyone who competes in the games goes into strict training. They do it to get a crown that will not last; but we do it to get a crown that will last forever. Therefore I do not run like a man running aimlessly; I do not fight like a man beating the air. No, I beat my body and make it my slave so that after I have preached to others, I myself will not be disqualified for the prize. 1 Corinthians 9: 24-27

In this passage of Scripture, Paul is reminding the Church that victory is never without cost. Excellence is never easy. To be successful in anything requires a tremendous amount of discipline. When we hear that word—discipline—many of us still automatically think of a dad's belt, or standing in the corner in "time out," or getting the car keys or cell phone taken away. We equate discipline only with punishment. But, let's remember our new definition of discipline: bringing order to disorder in the mind, body and spirit.

People all over the world intuitively understand what it takes to excel at something. Businesspeople know it takes long hours to get ahead. Musicians know it takes hours a day of practice to become proficient. Educators spend much of their time becoming experts in their field. Farmers know there is no harvest without great toil, and so on. There is a cost to excellence. All great athletes, musicians, scientists and writers spend hour after hour, day after day, year after year becoming (and staying) excellent at what they do. But for all this, the payoff is just being very good at what they do and perhaps bringing enjoyment to others, something the

Apostle Paul referred to as "a crown that will not last."

Conversely, for a Christian, being disciplined means more of Jesus and less of oneself. There is no better trade!

I was an athlete as a child and spent about fifteen years deeply involved in sport. Everyone has the same amount of hours in the day, and for those years, a large portion of my given hours were spent pursuing this passion. Now, each year when we take out the Christmas decorations I find two large boxes in the corner and think, "What's in here?" Then I open one and remember: They are full of trophies, medals, ribbons, plaques and certificates that represent a large percentage of my life. Those thousands and thousands of hours of conditioning and competing now fit into two cardboard boxes—definitely crowns that will not last. I hope when my life is over and I stand before the Lord, I will have more to show for the life He gave me than a couple of cardboard boxes of awards.

There are two things that I am hoping to show you through this story of an athlete's dedication. The first is that, when a person loves what he does, it is a joy to spend as much time and energy as is possible in pursuing that end. The second is that we, as believers in the Lord Jesus Christ, need to approach our walk with Him with the dedication of an athlete. That is why Paul equates our efforts to those of an athlete or a soldier. It takes a lot of discipline, not just every now and then, but all the time, every day. That is why Jesus called His followers "disciples." Walking with Him requires laying down our own lives and agendas, taking up our cross and following Him.

I started to swim when I was five years old and quickly fell in love with the sport. At first we practiced two hours a day on weekdays and occasionally on Saturday mornings. I began competing and did pretty well. As I grew older, my passion for the sport increased. I worked very hard every day at practice and rarely missed a workout. I ran and did abdominal workouts on my own to increase my strength, and I followed a strict diet so as not to hurt my performance.

We moved to California when I was in high school and I joined a team there that trained at another level. Two hours became four, both before and after school, and even on Saturdays. So I began to set my alarm for 4:20 a.m. to be sure I had time to get to the pool by five. I often had trouble staying awake in my first class of the day, but I thought this schedule was awesome! I came home from practice in the evening, ate dinner and did a little homework with a goal of being in bed by 8:30. I didn't drink or smoke or do drugs, not because I had a godly conviction about them at that point in my life, but simply because I did not want anything to get in the way of my sport. I was dedicated, disciplined.

All of this hard work seemed to be paying off. I was swimming fast and college coaches were watching me, until one day the summer before my senior year when I was doing the crunch machine in the gym and suddenly felt all the muscles in my back wrench. I actually saw stars like in the cartoons. It turns out my body was really weak because I was coming down with a severe case of mononucleosis which laid me flat on my back for almost two weeks.

When it was over, I felt as though I had to learn to swim again. I was terrible in the water. Those days were horrible. Often I wanted to quit. I struggled through my senior year, performing far below where I had been. But I made it through, and still managed to obtain a scholarship with a Division I school in California.

I reported to my new university a couple of weeks early to start practicing with my new coach and team, almost exactly one year after being so sick. It was amazing. Suddenly my body remembered what it felt like to go fast, and I was even better than before. I was so glad I had not given up when I was feeling quite low. Then, all that really hard work and perseverance from the last year paid off. Continuing to do what I knew I must do, even when I could not immediately see great results, carried me through the difficult time.

I forgot to mention that I was recruited to swim the mile. Nobody aspires to swim the mile. It is such a long race and it hurts badly. But there I was, the miler, and I did really well my freshman year, placing third in our conference meet and qualifying for nationals and some world-class meets.

That was about the time I met two very significant people in my life: Jesus Christ and Eli Gautreaux. The first became my Savior and made my life whole; the second became my husband and best friend. For the first time in my life, I had a purpose greater than swimming. Surprisingly and almost instantaneously, the notion of chasing a black line on the bottom of a pool seemed so insignificant.

Jesus has a way (in case you don't already know) of taking our limited dreams and small ambitions and replacing them with something so much better and more consequential! Suddenly I found I was thinking about the Bible, and thinking about the new people in my life who were encouraging me to grow. Swimming became less and less important. I began to realize, for the first time in my life, what it meant to walk with the Lord, how to be a disciple of Christ and a daughter of the King.

Within the next year, Eli and I were at Sam Houston State University, having laid down our scholarships and our swimming ambitions altogether, beginning a little group there called Chi Alpha, a campus ministry for students. But God uses everything from our pasts to help us be effective in our futures, so the things we learned from being athletes still play a huge role in our lives as followers of Christ.

Remember the two points of this story: When a person loves something, he is glad to give his all to follow that thing. People all over the world intuitively understand what it takes to excel at something. I would never classify myself as an over-achiever. In fact, as a child I had a perpetually messy room and made consistently average grades in school. So it has challenged me to look back at that early time in my life and see how much of myself I gave to the pursuit I loved. As an athlete, I wanted to be the best I could be at my sport, and it affected everything I did: my diet, my schedule, my social life, everything. We know that there is a price to be paid for greatness, but when we love what we have given ourselves to, the price does not seem too great at all.

So why, as Christians, do so many of us resent the fact that Jesus asks for everything when we become His followers? Like committed athletes, Jesus asks us to be disciplined with everything—our minds, our time, our money, our actions—but many of us turn away sad, like the rich young ruler in the Bible (Luke 18), unwilling to lay down all of ourselves.

We need to adjust our thinking. Giving all these things to Jesus yields a life of incredible fulfillment, freedom and peace. Not only is this the healthiest way for us to live, but it is also the best way we can be a help and blessing to others. Jesus said we are a "city on a hill." People all around us will be affected by us as we walk with Him. They will see our lives shining with joy, peace and forgiveness, and will want to be a part. This is why we must be real disciples, really disciplined. We must be ready to minister and share the love, hope and healing that Jesus can bring to others.

As a swimmer I exercised careful discipline, knowing that every choice would affect my next performance, even if that competition was a month or more away. As believers we need to realize that our daily walk with the Lord is what prepares us for the future challenges of life—and there will be some massive challenges!

I told you about an illness that knocked me down in my sport for an entire year. How many things in my walk as a Christian have tried to knock me out of this race? It is sometimes a real struggle to walk in discipline as a believer. At times it can be so hard we want to quit, but we must not quit. The world needs us to be ready to minister and to share the hope and healing that Jesus brings. We must be ready at all times to share the hope that we have. We know there is a price to be paid for greatness, but when we love the One we have given ourselves to, Jesus, the price does not seem too great at all.

Application

Reflect on what thing or things in your life have been given your full attention and concern. For me it was swimming. What is it for you? It might be academics, music, exercise, video games, a relationship; any number of things. Think how you have shaped your life around that pursuit. (You might experiment with writing down your thoughts and reflections in a journal.)

What is your motive in that pursuit? A good question to define motive is to ask yourself, "Why do I do the things I do, and who do I do them for?" If the answer is for "myself and myself alone," then you can begin to realize that a particular pursuit might not be the best use of your time and energy. Perhaps you have been acting with selfish motives.

Next, consider how you could better use your time and energy to do something for God. How could you better help others through your time and effort? There could be several things you could purposefully do within that sport, field of study or activity that could be very helpful and lead many others to God.

Differentiate whether the thing you are pursuing is helping you grow closer to God or taking you further from Him. If it is keeping you from God, prayerfully consider laying down that pursuit or relationship. If you know that God is asking you to lay it down, quick obedience is important.

FOUR

What Stands in the Way

Now the Lord is the Spirit, and where the Spirit of the Lord is, there is freedom. And we, who with unveiled faces all reflect the Lord's glory, are being transformed into His likeness with ever-increasing glory, which comes from the Lord, who is the Spirit. 2 Corinthians 3: 17-18

As I write this, it is the first week of June, and at this time of the year many college students are back home, living with their parents again. Returning home often provides a shock to both students and parents, as it is very interesting to readjust to living under the same roof. It takes some work to come to an understanding when you have adult children and their parents living together.

Right now, there are college students everywhere wishing their mothers did not have quite as much interest in what they were doing and with whom. But, in their defense, moms cannot help but care. To a mom, it really does not seem that long ago that her now-grown child was a baby in diapers and helpless without her. Moms are wired to be concerned and protective of their kids. God designed them to be the glue that holds everything together—nurturing, encouraging, life-giving. There really is no way to over-emphasize their importance.

With that said, we all know that mothers sometimes get a bad rap. Some would say we are bossy, picky, impossible to satisfy, demanding, nagging; the list goes on and on. But what is it that moms want? I am certainly not saying that mothers are perfect, but deep down, moms simply want the very best for their children. They want them to have a happy childhood, a healthy mind and body, a great work ethic, and live up to their full potential. They want their kids to have an excellent future. And eventually moms want lots of terrific grandchildren.

Like moms, God oftentimes gets a really bad rap. There is no way to over-emphasize His importance. He truly is The Life-Giver! People accuse Him of being bossy, demanding, impossible to satisfy, nagging; all those things. But what is it that God wants for us?

Simply this: We are His children and He wants the best for us. He wants us to be healthy in mind, body and spirit, and to be happy and content. He wants us to be free from the baggage of foolish, selfish choices. He wants us to live to achieve our full potential. And He wants us to make as many spiritual children and grandchildren as we can. He wants all of us to have an excellent future with Him in heaven for all eternity.

However, we are fallen from what He created us to be. Our very nature is sinful, and we are prone to terrible choices, thoughts and mistakes. God knows this, of course, and He has a plan. Part of the provision of the cross is healing and wholeness, even for our spirits. God, through Christ, makes us righteous. When we are born again, it is Christ Himself who lives in us.

Referring back to the passage in 2 Corinthians, when we ask Jesus to live in our hearts, we begin the journey of being transformed into His likeness with ever-increasing glory. Transformed into His likeness, Christ's likeness. This is the whole of Christianity; this is exactly what it is all about. Christianity is not about politics, red states or blue states. It is not about hospitals or education or programs. It is about drawing men and women unto Christ, in Whose presence they will be transformed into His image. This is

God's hope and dream for each of us, that we would rest in Him as Jesus rests in Him, have perfect fellowship with Him as Jesus does, think like Jesus and act like Jesus, that we would reflect the image of God, to a hurting and desperate world now, and forever in heaven.

Equally astounding is the cold, hard fact that there is only one thing—much like Superman's kryptonite—that can stop us from becoming more like Christ. Just one thing, and that is ourselves. Not terrorists or bombs or governments or anyone else. Just ourselves.

Let's take a look at three of the most common, self-inflicted pitfalls that keep us from growing in the grace and knowledge of Christ, and what we can do to recognize them and avoid them.

Laziness

I will never cease to be amazed at my own capacity for laziness. It is tremendous. This is the mindset that says, "Wait a minute, I never wanted to be Mother Theresa or Billy Graham. I just want to be an ordinary Christian, not a saint." We are much too easily contented to stay where we are. This current me is so much better than the old me; surely that is good enough. But the key here is that "good enough" is just a shadow, never a reality.

Paul expresses this perfectly with his athletic imagery in 1 Corinthians 9: 24-27:

> "Do you not know that in a race all the runners run, but only one gets the prize? Run in such a way as to get the prize. Everyone who competes in the games goes into strict training. They do it to get a crown that will not last; but we do it to get a crown that will last forever. Therefore I do not run like a man running aimlessly; I do not fight like a man beating the air. No, I beat my body and make it my slave so that after I have preached to others, I myself will not be disqualified for the prize."

This is so true of athletics and fitness, of musical talent, of study—anything. If we are not advancing, we are regressing. If we are not moving forward, then we are sliding backwards. Paul says, "run, strict training, beat my body." It is pushing, moving, doing, going. Not passive Christianity, but very active. Studying, thinking, praying, worshipping, witnessing, evangelizing; we are to strive to have a very active walk with the Lord.

Our goodness can never be good enough. We must always be growing in God's goodness. Christ's perfection is so complete and so amazing, we have forever to keep moving in that direction. The best is yet to come!

Fear

Some of us are afraid of anything and everything. My kids used to like to jump out and scare me when I was coming down the hall, and it worked every time. We all like to be sure; we like to be aware and ready; we like to be in control. Fear, then, is a major deterrent to spiritual growth.

We can sometimes be like the kid who has a toothache. He knows he can go to his mother and tell her, and she will give him medicine to deaden the pain. But he also knows she will call the dentist and make an appointment, which can be much worse than a toothache. So, no thanks, he chooses to suffer in silence.

We are just the same way with God. We have some sort of pain in our life, often a recurring one, but we know if we go to Him for help, He is very likely to put His finger on the real cause of the pain and ask us to deal with it. My heart is broken, again; yes, but what is the real issue? I am trapped in an eating disorder; yes, but what is the real issue, the one in my heart?

Remember the goal here: to transform us into people like Christ who can shine brightly and hugely impact this broken world with love and hope, and then spend forever together with Him in heaven. Remember the kryptonite. The only thing that can stop

God from doing this, from making me like Christ, is myself and my own stubborn will. Isn't fear really an indicator of a lack of trust? We know God has our best interest in mind, we know He knows best. So let Him operate away.

"And so we know and rely on the love God has for us. God is love. Whoever lives in love lives in God, and God in Him. In this way, love is made complete among us so that we may have confidence on the day of judgment, because in this world we are like Him. There is no fear in love. But perfect love drives out fear" (1 John 4: 16-18).

Don't be afraid! Trust in God's perfect love.

Disobedience/Rebellion

This last thing is a much tougher obstacle to overcome. Rebellion and disobedience are such a deeply rooted part of our old, sinful selves. We want to be on the throne of our own heart and life; therefore, we must die to self every day in order to give God His rightful place in our lives as king.

Our perspective on obedience is often so fickle. We totally understand and agree with the need for it when it comes to others, especially those who are accountable to us, such as our kids, people at work, and so on. Of course obedience is important. But how real and frequent is the thought, "You can't tell me what to do!" when it comes to us being obedient? We really think we know what is best, even though we concede that our perspective is so limited. God has, literally, an infinitely better perspective on all things. He knows best.

Again it comes down to trust. Do we trust God? Do we believe He knows what He is talking about when He asks us to do something like lay down a bad habit, pick up a good habit, talk to someone, pray for someone, witness to someone, change a job or major, not to say everything we think? We should trust that He knows what is best for us and just do it. One simple definition is this:

Obedience is doing exactly what I am told, and doing it quickly, because I love and trust Him[4]. As soon as God asks something, I will do it because I love and trust Him.

In thinking about obedience and choices, a mental picture that has helped me is of a series of doors and hallways. Each choice we make opens up a whole new set of doors and opportunities, for good or for bad. God has a dream for each of us, and He knows what our greatest potential really is. If we were perfectly obedient every time, each act of obedience would lead us through one door that would lead to another door, and so on, all the way to Christlikeness.

Conversely, each act of disobedience closes a door, hindering our progress. God can work all things for good, absolutely. But what are we missing by choosing disobedience? What amazing things could we have experienced in the Lord if only we had said, "Yes"?

How do we overcome laziness, fear and disobedience? Recognize them for what they really are—kryptonite to our growth in God. Tricks, traps and stumbling blocks that keep us from being transformed into Christ's image. God has a plan to make us like Christ, to make us ready for heaven. Let Him do it. The only thing that can stop Him from doing it is us.

1 Peter 3: 15 says, "But in your hearts revere Christ as Lord. Always be prepared to give an answer to everyone who asks you to give the reason for the hope that you have." We want to always be ready to share the love and hope of God with others. Ready spiritually, physically, and in every other way. Choice by choice, obedience by obedience, God wants to make us into beacons of light and hope for the people all around us, into men and women who can change the world with the love and hope of Christ.

Application

No matter how long we have been walking with Jesus—whether it be a week, a year, a decade, or since we were young children—we should be progressing in our understanding of, and obedience to, God. Reflect on your current walk with God. Can you gauge that you are further along in knowledge, obedience, hunger and love for God and others than you ever have been, or is there a time in your life you feel you were further along than you are currently?

Spend some time honestly considering this in thought and prayer. If you feel a regression has occurred, consider what could be the cause. Examine and evaluate your heart in light of the three obstacles of laziness, fear and disobedience, and ask God to help you overcome and move forward.

FIVE

Surrender

Recently we attended the music recital of a young friend who had come to the university for a week to study piano. It was our first time to sit in that particular recital hall, and it was truly lovely. Warm wood along the ceiling and walls, soft lighting, and a gorgeous grand piano on center stage—the whole room created a sense of anticipation and excitement for what was to come.

The lights dimmed, the stage door opened, and out walked the pianist. Calm, confidant, expectant, he sat down on the bench and began.

I am always amazed to watch a master play. Whatever the instrument, the expert musician can coax mood and melody and emotion out of a piece of wood or metal that is truly beautiful. His face glows with delight, his upper body moves with the music, and the instrument responds with perfection. It comes alive, and everyone listening marvels at something so fully and completely doing what it was created to do.

That same piano could sit there all day and not make a sound without the direction and leading of a skilled player. It could plink out a very thin version of "Chopsticks" or "Three Blind Mice" at the hands of an amateur. Worse, it could make a terrible, discordant racket at the hands of someone completely unqualified. The best thing for a beautiful piano is for it to be played by a master.

Romans 12: 1-2 says, "Therefore, I urge you, brothers and sisters, in view of God's mercy, to offer your bodies as a living sacrifice, holy and pleasing to God—this is your true and proper worship. Do not conform to the pattern of this world, but be transformed by the renewing of your mind. Then you will be able to test and approve what God's will is—His good, pleasing and perfect will."

This passage challenges us to give our all to God—body, will, intellect and devotion—our entire lives. Just like the grand piano, our lives can be "played" by many people. Who better to orchestrate a life than the very One who made it and who knows exactly what it is capable of doing?

Each of us have just two choices in life. The first is to keep letting the world play us. We can drift along and let life happen, pretending that we are the ruler of our own life, the king or queen on the throne of our own hearts. We can be afraid to trust God. We can refuse to surrender anything to God, and let our moods and feelings and circumstances dictate our actions. This kind of life results in chaos and discord. It sounds like a terrible mess because it is a terrible mess; so much potential wasted.

The excellent choice is to let the Master play. He is the One who made us; He is the One who knows best and can see perfectly where we have come from and where we are going. He is truly the most qualified to run our lives. He can take everything He fashioned inside of each of us and use it for the highest good of others, and, more importantly, for His glory. We must choose to let Him transform us into His own image, as we were created to be.

The very word "surrender" implies a choice made. When two armies are fighting, the carnage will continue until one side says, "We give up!" As long as there is life and breath, surrender is an act of the will, a choice. Daily surrender is a discipline. This should be comforting and encouraging to us. We can surrender control of our lives to God and be happy knowing that we do not have to become perfect overnight. In fact, many of us would probably implode if we became perfect overnight! We have spent way too much time living in the kingdom of darkness and have a lot of selfishness, bad habits and wrong thinking to wade through. God is patient, and gently helps us become more like Jesus day by day, year by year. We just have to surrender and obey each thing God asks of us.

Once Eli and I were at a church youth group graduation service. After the service was over, one of the graduates came up to greet us, accompanied by his little brother. This child was adorable. It was a cowboy church, and he was certainly a cowboy in the making. He had his boots polished, his belt buckle gleaming, and his hat brushed. The thing that struck me most, however, was the enormous Lego truck he was holding in his arms. It was a model of an eighteen-wheeler; he had built this truck all by himself.

Now, this little guy was five years old at the most, holding on to a huge model truck! I was impressed! I sat beside him and asked how he was able to build such a thing.

He set down the truck and pulled out a big packet of papers from his mother's handbag. It was the instruction manual that came with the truck, laid out in pictures so someone his age could understand it. On page one was a picture of one block, page two showed two blocks, page three had three blocks, and so on. All the child had to do was put one block down at a time, then turn the page to see where to put the next one.

Walking with God is just like that! Day by day, choice by choice, obedience by obedience, we are being transformed into the beautiful image of Jesus.

It seems so hard to let go of the control of our lives. It feels disconcerting and even scary to let someone else make the calls on what we do. We are anxious when we feel out of control of our lives. Anxiety is a strong mixture of fear, loss of control and doubt. The dictionary defines it as a feeling of worry, nervousness or unease, typically about an imminent event or something with an uncertain outcome. Since so many of us are feeling this way about our lives, it is actually great news that someone wants to help us. Not just any old someone, but God Himself! He can see infinitely better than we can. He made us and knows our full potential. He can see what needs to go and what needs to be enhanced. He is the most gracious and accurate surgeon who has ever lived, and we can trust Him.

Giving up control and surrendering our lives to God means becoming dependent on Him, and this has two facets.

First, we recognize what is true: We cannot exist without Him. We are dependent upon Him for everything we have. When we realize this fact, it is actually humorous that we try to hold on to the control of our lives. Where are we going to find our next breath, and how are we going to assure our next heartbeat? God knit us together in our mothers' wombs, and He breathed the breath of life into each of us. Surrendering to Him is just acknowledging the control He already has.

The second piece is that we truly can depend on Him. He is always faithful, and never fails. Life certainly may not be easy or pretty or without suffering; nowhere at all does the Bible say that becoming a Christian means life is going to be easy forever. What it means is that God will be with us every step of the way. He will help us through the toughest times and through the darkest nights. This is the beauty and the mystery of Christianity: There can be real joy and peace even in the middle of terrible circumstances and situations. God helps us and strengthens us and allows us to thrive inwardly no matter what is happening outwardly.

God is like a master concert pianist. He can hold our lives in His hands and use them for His great glory. All that is required of us is surrender. It is like when my girls were little and we took them to the pool to learn to swim. Eli would put his hand under their backs and tell them to relax and lay back flat on top of the water. Of course, they did not want to at first; it feels very much like you are going to sink to the bottom of the pool. But they trusted him and let him hold them up until they learned to do it all by themselves.

Relax in God's hands. Lose yourself in Him that you might truly find yourself (Matt. 10:39). Surrender the tight grip of control on your life and let Him transform your life from chaotic mess into a beautiful symphony.

Application

A prayer of surrender:

Lord Jesus, I surrender my life to You. Please change me. Take my life and make me what You created me to be. Make me more like You, Lord, so I can represent You well to the lost and hurting people in my life. Pour out the fruit of Your Holy Spirit in my life, so I can be Your hands and feet extended to my family, friends and neighbors. I want to live a life that makes a difference in this world, and I know I can only do that through You. Thank You for who You are, and for loving me. It is in the strong name of Jesus that I pray. Amen.

As we reach a place of truly surrendering our lives to God, we are ready to learn to walk in spiritual discipline—not because it is a duty, but because we truly love Jesus and want to be with Him and be more like Him. Keep on reading to learn how to walk with God all the days of your life, and how to change the world with the love and hope of Jesus.

SIX

Can It Really Be that Simple?

One of the greatest tragedies in life is watching a follower of Jesus give up and check himself out of the race. Many people find it very difficult to give up their own will over things and surrender everything to Him, and plenty of others never acquire the understanding of how to become strong enough to withstand the inevitable hardships of life. G.K. Chesterton said it best: "The Christian ideal has not been tried and found wanting; it has been found difficult and left untried."

Difficult in the sense of being wholly life-changing, yes. But being an effective and faithful follower of Christ is not impossible, nor is the way to become a solid and mature follower of Christ a secret. One of my favorite movie scenes of all time is in the film *National Treasure*, when the character Benjamin Gates finally realizes he literally has been holding the key to finding the treasure the whole time. Standing in the dusty and disappointing antechamber, he looks back and forth from the key to the lock on the wall and says, "Can it really be that simple?" The dialogue ends for a few minutes, and we watch with growing amazement as the key in his possession unlocks the door to a treasure far beyond anyone's ability to imagine.

Yes, it really is that simple. There are a few basic but foundational principles which the Lord has revealed, and everyone who understands and applies these things has a much easier time resisting the schemes of the enemy, who endeavors to destroy each and every one of us. Not only do these principles help us resist falling into traps of sin, deception and despair, but they also open the door to real and abundant life, true Christianity.

So many Christians who really love Jesus and want to serve Him never get past the drudgery of trying to follow a self-imposed list of do's and don'ts. That is not what Jesus meant when He promised abundant life! He wants to give peace and joy and fullness—real life, full of hope and purpose—like the massive treasure chamber that stretches on and on at the end of *National Treasure*. These principles can be simplified into three convictions every believer needs to make a priority of practicing and teaching in every stage of life.

A Real Devotional Life

If every Christian understood the principle of a true devotional life, the world would be a very different place. Some people brush it aside as unnecessary, others have good intentions yet never follow through, while many more entirely misunderstand the concept.

Oftentimes, we unwittingly project the idea that people must come to the large group meetings to be fed. The not-so-subtle insinuation is that the minister or teacher is the only one qualified to teach us and help us grow. Logically following this idea is the fallacy that one cannot properly feed himself. Of course, that is not at all true. It was never meant to be the pastor's job to carry every one of his flock on his back until heaven. It is one thing for a baby to be dependent on parents to feed him with a bottle, but another

CAN IT REALLY BE THAT SIMPLE?

thing altogether for a grown man or woman to still need someone to administer the bottle, lest they starve. We must learn to feed ourselves daily if we want to grow in the grace and knowledge of God.

The basic elements of a healthy devotional life include prayer and study. If your prayer life is nonexistent, set some goals for yourself and be disciplined to reach them. For example, make a pledge to pray for ten minutes every day. Write a list of people and things to pray for, and stick to it. You will be amazed that once you do this for a few days, ten minutes will not be enough. Prayer seems difficult and maybe even boring until you really do it and find that you are not just talking to yourself; God is with you and He is speaking to you.

Not only that, but praying for others is the often-overlooked key to building real love and relationship with them. God really does supernatural things when we pray. When we begin to honor the Lord's presence, the concept of praying without ceasing becomes easier to understand and achieve. Foster an attitude of thankfulness throughout the day. God is so good, and often we miss hundreds of opportunities to recognize His faithfulness in our lives. Strive to put your mind on Him all day, every day and it will change your life.

Study is much more than occasional reading. It is a deep engagement of the mind. Dig into the Bible. Pick a section of the Old Testament to read, or try reading the whole New Testament at a stretch, or just read the whole book from cover to cover. Set goals for reading the Word and discipline yourself to achieve them. Try reading Bible commentaries: your depth of understanding will be greatly increased. Read books written by the saints through the ages who have lived and walked with God before us. Their wisdom, understanding and experience is there on record to edify the body of Christ today.

Stretch your mind. Think deeply about the Lord, about His

character, His Word and His promises. Think in terms of an athlete. No one can approach the pull-up bar for the first time and do twenty pull-ups. But with training, conditioning, time and discipline, one pull-up gives way to two, then four, and eventually the twenty that seemed so impossible becomes a reality.

We are not called to be an ignorant and brainless body of believers; we can have the mind of Christ! Step by step, day by day, we build ourselves up in faith and understanding through a disciplined and purposeful devotional life.

Real Brotherhood

When we begin the journey as a follower of Christ, we need some help along the way. Real friends are the people who will walk along beside us as we follow Christ together; people who will love us enough to tell us the truth and redirect us, if need be, but who will also encourage us as we seek to live how God asks us to live.

Of course, we don't abandon our friends who are not believers; hopefully they will see and hear what God has done in our lives and seek Him also. But true fellowship needs to come from real friends who will help us walk with the Lord. Friends who will lift up and encourage; who will make us think about God because of the great conversations we have together; who will be a reminder of the way we are striving to live. This is true brotherhood.

As we mature, real brotherhood remains an imperative. Many Christians—pastors included—fail and fall for a lack of true friends. There often comes a point as we go further in our walk with the Lord when we can deceive ourselves into thinking there is no one who is able, willing or qualified to help us. This is nothing but pride. We have no one to help us only when we refuse to trust our brothers and sisters. The church is stifled and rendered almost impotent when mature believers refuse to love and trust one another. Just as in nature, the one who is alone, isolated and sick is the easiest one to be picked off by a predator. Too many believers and even church leaders have fallen because they had no one to trust and be honest with about their struggles.

As we grow in maturity in the Lord, there will never be a lack of people we can pour into, teach, challenge and encourage. At the same time, we will always need brothers and sisters who can tell us the truth, encourage and redirect us, if need be.

Not only that, but it is a biblical truth that iron sharpens iron; we are better together than we are alone. How much do we in the Church (and all those around us) miss out on when we refuse to walk in trust, honor and community with other Christians? Alone, a believer can be a lovely representation of Christ, yes; but together we become a mighty beacon of light and hope to the world—truly a city on a hill whose light cannot be hidden and whose presence acts as a magnet, compelling the lost to come home. No matter what stage of life we are in, we need to love, honor and trust one another in real, godly friendships.

Real Responsibility

Throughout many years of being a college minister, I have seen one summertime story play out too often in the lives of students.

He may have been the most responsible person in the whole dorm, managing to be an effective discipleship group leader, making great grades, holding a part-time job, even keeping his laundry neatly put away. But this young man might find it is very attractive to fall into the old habits of childhood during summer break and become a whiny, lazy, selfish child again. When the responsibility of caring for others stops, the growth in character regresses. His mom might do everything for him out of sheer force of habit, but the truth is that everyone knows it is gross for a twenty-one-year-old to sleep until noon every day, shove dirty dishes under the bed and wait until his mother does the laundry for him. It is not difficult to see that something is very undesirable about that scenario.

It is the same way in our walk with the Lord, whether we are twenty or forty or sixty. We must have some real responsibility or we will not only stop growing, we will actually begin to regress. There is a misconception in the Church today that being committed and having responsibility means simply having a job or a task, like unlocking the doors, or running the computers, or being a part of the worship team. These things are important, but they are not the kind of responsibility that will grow a person into a mature believer.

We must never take lightly the great responsibility everyone of has for people: to win souls. Our job as believers, the very thing that will make us grow up and be unselfish, is to share the good news with the people in our sphere of influence, to teach them how to walk with the Lord and how to pass everything on to someone else.

We must always be mindful of the people around us. It is no accident that you are rubbing shoulders with the people you find yourself around at this time. Minister to them, serve them, share your faith with them, pray for them, fight for them, honor them, love them. Do unto them as you would do unto the Lord. Very few people wander into relationship with Jesus on their own, and it is not just the pastor's job to bring people in; it is our responsibility, too.

When a follower of Christ accepts this great responsibility, not only will many people be brought into the kingdom, but that person will find himself growing in his own relationship with the Lord in ways that would have been impossible otherwise.

Many of us sit in churches all of our lives without ever understanding or accepting the concept of individual responsibility. We look and see the many empty seats around us, and often blame

CAN IT REALLY BE THAT SIMPLE?

to the preacher or the worship team or the facility itself for not doing enough to attract and keep new people. We hide behind ecclesiastical busyness, contenting ourselves to feel like we are doing something through our many meetings and tasks, selfishly refusing to look and see our responsibility to win the lost and disciple them. We point to the church sign on the street and say to ourselves that everyone can plainly see the time church starts; it is their own fault if they never come.

But that simply is not the way it works. Very infrequently a person is brought to the feet of Jesus by a dream or vision, but the vast majority of the time, people are brought to the Lord by faithful disciples like Andrew who consistently brought people to meet the Messiah. Responsibility for others and to God's kingdom is an essential factor of true Christianity.

Yes, it really is that simple. A real devotional life, real brotherhood and real responsibility are the key components of a life well spent in serving Jesus. When we incorporate these three areas into our own lives, teach those under our care how to have these three things, and also teach them how to pass them on to another generation, then we are well on our way to the abundant and fruitful life Jesus offers to us and to the world around us.

Application

In your journal, reflect on the following thoughts:

What does my current devotional life look like on a daily, weekly and monthly basis? What is one step I can take daily this week to have a stronger devotional life?

Do I have real brothers/sisters in my life? Are there people in my life who regularly encourage and lift one another up, who inspire me to think through great conversations about God, and who are a reminder of the way I am striving to live? If yes, list them and pray for them. If no, let God speak to you about who this could be and where you should go to find them.

Do I have kingdom responsibility in my life? Am I accepting the responsibility to help someone else know God? If yes, ask God to give you new vision and wisdom for them. If no, ask God to help you embrace that responsibility for your family, coworkers, fellow students and neighbors.

SEVEN

Self-Control

I have been in the habit of keeping a journal for nearly twenty years. A few years ago, I read through some of the earliest volumes and had a terrible revelation. I noticed there were several things I continually complained about in the pages of my journals, entry after entry.

I am sure many people struggle with the same things I wrote about, like laziness, for example (Why don't I do what I want to do?), or with losing and gaining back the same fifteen pounds about twenty times. After a while, I began to feel embarrassed as I realized I basically had my journal entries memorized. The journals for the first few years were the same: absolutely nothing changed because of my pitiful lack of self-control.

What is self-control? One simple definition is consistently disciplined choices. Everything we say, do and think is the direct result of a choice we have made in our hearts. As followers of Christ, we must learn to be disciplined in our choices and actions so our lives properly reflect God. Remember, God does not just have self-control, He is self-control. He always chooses rightly.

Undisciplined lives are often a mess, both outwardly and inwardly, and that is a terrible, pathetic and inaccurate reflection of God to show the world.

What does this mean? Well, it means self-control requires more than just making some good choices one time. It requires constant, daily discipline to stick to these choices, no matter what. It is not enough to have good intentions about something. After all, a person can intend to eat right and exercise, even reading several books and becoming quite knowledgeable on the subject, and still be fifty pounds overweight. You have to make good choices and then act on them consistently.

We are called disciples of Jesus, a word that is so closely related to the word discipline. Yet, that is the very thing we all lack! Discipline comes from daily choices—being prepared to make a good choice ahead of time, and being strong enough to stick to that choice when the time comes.

We are able to control ourselves. The Lord in His mercy even provides greater help with this area, as self-control is a fruit of His Spirit. He will help us to be disciplined, to make wise choices, and have self-control. All we need to do is ask, and then exercise our muscle of discipline.

In Galatians 5:17, Paul says, "For the sinful nature desires what is contrary to the Spirit, and the Spirit what is contrary to the sinful nature. They are in conflict with each other, so that you do not do what you want."

But in verse 24 he says, "Those who belong to Jesus Christ have crucified the sinful nature with its passions and desires. Since we live by the Spirit, let us keep in step with the Spirit." We must discipline ourselves to heed the voice of the Spirit and not the voice of our own sinful nature.

Benjamin Franklin said, "Who is strong? He that can conquer his bad habits." This is true. We, through the infinite power of the Holy Spirit, can conquer our bad habits. It is a shame when

Christians allow themselves to be caught in the same unhealthy, ungodly habits year after year. After all, the many outward signs of an undisciplined life are actually reflections of our lack of spiritual discipline. When we listen to our sinful nature and not the Spirit, we are really telling the Lord that we know far better how to run our lives and our business than He does. We are proving that we just do not care what He says or thinks.

It is painful to realize this, but it is true. The reality is that all of our lives belong to God, not just the parts we think should belong to Him. He bought and paid for all of us on the cross, which means He owns our mouths and our waistlines, He owns our money and our things, He owns our sexuality and He owns our moods. When we choose to follow our own sinful natures, we are denying His Lordship of our lives. By allowing myself to be stuck in these areas of my flesh, I am denying the power of God in my life, denying myself the pleasure and enrichment that comes with growing in the Lord, and denying my neighbors the benefit of a more godly friend.

But learning to walk in self-control can feel like the man standing in a dark room who tries to force out the darkness with his arms. All the pushing, shoving and struggling in the world will not push out the darkness. Darkness will only leave the room when the man turns on the light. How much easier would it be if, instead of struggling with bad habits year after year, we replaced them with good habits?

This actually brings up the two ways of looking at self-control.

The Things I Do

These are the disciplines we incorporate into our lives and practice on a regular basis. These are the activities I make sure are a regular part of my life. For example, taking time to read and pray and study—actually practicing a real and healthy devotional life. Not just talking about it, or just knowing that I ought to have one, but truly practicing a devotional life. This means that I set my alarm and get out of bed and sit with my Bible at the kitchen table where I will read and think and pray while I drink a cup of coffee every morning. If and when I have to be at work early, I will set my alarm even earlier so I can still have time for devotion.

This is the way I prioritize being a part of the Body of Christ above all else. I choose my location and ministry first, then find a job that allows me time to spend investing in people. I choose what church and home group meetings I will be a part of first, then arrange the rest of my schedule around them.

Every week, every month, every year, I make decisions with my money. I will give at least a tithe (ten percent of my income) to my church and then above and beyond that to faithfully support missionary work across the globe. I will be generous with my time and my money to my neighbors, so that they know I love and care for them. I will choose to live simply so that I have plenty of money and time to be generous with.

I choose to put positive things into my life and mind. I will listen to the kind of music that uplifts and encourages me. I will read books, magazines or websites that edify and strengthen me. I will eat food because it is healthy and good for me, and I will eat only as much of it as I need.

These are the things I will do even when I do not feel like it; especially when I do not feel like it. These are my habits, and as I once read on a motivational poster long ago, my habits are the things that build my character, and my character is what impacts my destiny.

One thing that is needed to impact my habits is some fortitude. Look at the definition for fortitude: courage, bravery, endurance, resilience, mettle, moral fiber, strength of mind, strength of character, strong-mindedness, backbone, spirit, grit. I love that last word, *grit*. This is what we need as followers of Jesus, and this is how we need to approach the things we do in life. We need grit to stay the course even when things are tough. We need grit to stay the course precisely because things are going to get tough. Jesus said, "In this world you will have trouble. But take courage, for I have overcome the world!" (John 16:33).

This is why we practice disciplined lives. The world is tough, but in Jesus we can be even tougher than the world. This is why soldiers get up and run in formation and with heavy gear every day. When I was growing up on the submarine bases we lived on, and was getting into the car to go to 5 a.m. swim practice, the Marines on base had already been up and running for some time. They did their drills and exercises every day, rain or shine, because they needed to be ready when the battle got real and the bullets were flying. Self-control is taking control of my daily choices, decisions and habits that build my life so I am always ready for whatever life brings.

The Things I Do Not Do

These are also disciplines. These are the things in my life I have set clear boundaries around, and that no matter what circumstances arise and no matter who tries to change my mind, I will not do these things.

Have you ever seen the movie *Chariots of Fire*? You should watch it, or watch it again; it is so good! It tells the story of two different Olympic runners. One, named Eric Liddell, is a strong Christian and later becomes a missionary. He has a conviction not to run on the Sabbath day, and acts on that conviction even though it means missing his Olympic chance in that event. It is such a powerful testimony!

The things we will not do are just as important as the things we do. It is important that we be careful not to become legalistic here. The Bible is clear that we are all to work out our own salvation (Phil. 2: 12-13). In other words, we cannot judge other people who have different habits and convictions than ours. With that said, these things we will not do are important to the foundation of our lives and to building our character.

There is true freedom and safety in establishing healthy boundaries in our lives. We will never, ever have to deal with causing a drunk-driving accident if we never take a sip of alcohol. We will never have to deal with the life-long repercussions of an out-of-wedlock pregnancy if we do not sleep with people who are not our spouse. We will never have to deal with the devastating effects of pornography if we never look at pornography. We will never be buried under crushing debt if we never spend more than we have. We will never have to deal with the awful health problems that come with obesity if we never become overweight. These things are just logical truths. Good, healthy boundaries yield good, healthy lives.

Not doing things takes a lot of resolve, too. When we live like Christians (a word that actually means people who act like Christ), we will really stand out. Actually, we will stand out like a sore thumb, and this is not always fun or easy. This is why the things we will not do have to be decided in advance. When peer pressure is on and people are ridiculing us for something, it would be much too easy to just give in unless we have already made the choice.

The more we stick to our convictions, the easier it becomes to stay true to them. If we spend fifty years of life eating right and exercising regularly, we are very unlikely to let it all go and gain a hundred pounds. If we never entertain the idea of being unfaithful to our spouses or allow ourselves to be put into a situation where that is likely to happen, we will most likely never be unfaithful to our spouses. Habits are strong and hard to break, even good habits.

Remember, God is discipline! He is self-control. He is not asking of us anything He has not already provided the means to do. God always chooses rightly, and He gives us the ability to do likewise. Setting healthy boundaries for ourselves makes our lives steadier and more effective. Fortitude builds habits, which builds character, which leads to our destiny. Amazingly, a paradox of the Christian faith is that when I give God more control of my life, I find that my self-control increases. A great place to start building healthy habits is to ask God to help us develop the fruit of His Spirit. Then, when He asks us to do something, to do it.

Application

One exercise we learned from our friend Harvey Herman, author of *Discipleship by Design*, and have used for many years with student leaders, is that of making purposes and goals for our lives.

A purpose is a "To Be" statement. For example, "I want to be a woman of prayer." A goal is a "To Do" statement. For example, "In order to become a woman of prayer, I will start by praying ten minutes a day for three weeks straight."

Purposes can be broad and about anything at all: physical, spiritual or mental. Goals need to be measurable in time and duration otherwise they will not go very far. When you have accomplished your goal, then set it again and make some more until these become your life habits.

Spend some time making yourself a list of Purposes and Goals that will help you establish several new healthy habits in your life. (Do at least one for each area, but be careful not to try to do too many at once.)

Things I Will Do:
A healthy habit I will incorporate into my daily routine.

Purpose:

Goal:

SELF-CONTROL

Things I Will Not Do:
A new boundary I will establish in my life.

Purpose:

Goal:

EIGHT

Building Blocks for a Healthy Spiritual Life

One of the most helpful books in learning to walk in discipline as a Christian is called *Celebration of Discipline* by Richard Foster. We have used this book in leadership training for years, and find that it opens eyes to some of the most tried-and-true spiritual disciplines practiced by Christians throughout Church history. I recommend you read the book and consider its points the building blocks of your "workout regimen" as a Christian.

We have already addressed the point that if we are not moving forward in our faith, we are certainly falling backwards. There is no such thing as maintaining spiritual health without consistent healthy practices. With that in mind, let's take a brief look at each of the twelve disciplines outlined in Foster's book.

The Inward Disciplines: Meditation, Prayer, Fasting, Study

These are the disciplines that we practice on our own—in our own life and on our own time. No one else can do these for us. If we practice these regularly, we will be strong and ready for anything life throws our way; if we do not practice them, we will be weak and easily knocked down.

First is *meditation*. This word has been hijacked in our thinking by practices of Eastern mysticism, but it is actually a healthy part of our spiritual workout. Meditation is simply thinking deeply on the things of God: about the truth that we have read in the Word, about the nature and character of God and His Kingdom. It is taking the time to process and evaluate, letting the things we are learning truly seep into our lives and become a part of who we are and how we think.

Christians are to love God with all their hearts, souls and minds (Matt. 22:37). We were never called to be mindless and brainless. Rather than seeking to empty ourselves of everything (as Eastern mysticism tradition teaches), Christian mediation seeks to fill us with the thoughts and wisdom of God. Meditation, thinking deeply about the things of God, plays a big part in loving God with our minds.

Next is *prayer*, which is something that Christians talk about all the time. We tell each other we will pray and ask one another to pray. We pray over our food; we pray before sporting events. We pray when things seem to be going wrong.

But what is prayer, and why is it such a big deal? Simply stated, prayer is important because God desires to have fellowship with us, and wants us to learn to trust Him as the source of everything we need. He is all-good, all-powerful and all-knowing, and through prayer we begin to develop the habit of looking to Him in all situations.

In Luke 11: 9-13, we read Jesus' words:

> So I say to you: Ask and it will be given to you; seek and you will find; knock and the door will be opened to you. For everyone who asks receives; the one who seeks finds; and to the one who knocks, the door will be opened. Which of

you fathers, if your son asks for a fish, will give him a snake instead? Or if he asks for an egg, will give him a scorpion? If you then, though you are evil, know how to give good gifts to your children, how much more will your Father in heaven give the Holy Spirit to those who ask Him!

Prayer, in essence, is a conversation between us and God. We speak to Him, pour our hearts and cares out to Him, bring our needs and desires to Him and the most beautiful thing is, God also speaks to us! Prayer is a healthy part of every Christian's day. It is not just something we do at a worship service or at the dinner table, but a discipline we can put into practice any time and any place. In fact, in I Thessalonians 5: 16-18, Paul exhorts believers to "rejoice always, pray continually, give thanks in all circumstances; for this is God's will for you in Christ Jesus."

Prayer is so much more than just uttering a few words before a meal or before sleep. It is real fellowship and communion with God. He speaks, comforts, encourages, directs and teaches us through prayer. We can pour out our deepest secrets, desires and hopes to Him, and He hears us. It is through prayer that we can ask for forgiveness and receive it.

Daily, consistent prayer changes us—and it truly does bring change to the people and places we pray for. If you do not have a prayer life, start with something easy, like ten minutes a day, and go from there. You will soon be able to look back and see the incredible strength it affords in your life.

More than just a conversation, prayer is a conduit through which the wisdom, blessings and power of God can flow in and through our lives. Prayer is not to be just an afterthought or a life preserver in times of trouble; it can actually become our sustenance. But to get there, we must begin somewhere. Right now is a great time!

Third on the list of inward disciplines is *fasting*. This often makes people think of Mahatma Ghandhi after a hunger strike, which seems too hard and scary. Isn't it unhealthy to go without food? Well, no, not for most of us! Truly, one of the best things we can learn as a Christian is how to tell ourselves no. *Fasting* is a way to remind ourselves and our sinful nature that God is the boss, not our stomachs. Throughout the Bible and Church history, many people practiced this discipline of fasting—specifically going without food to focus more intently on prayer and fellowship with God. Jesus Himself fasted in the desert for an extended period of time, and anything He did is good for us to do, as well.

We do not like to fast for so many reasons. We are much too devoted to our own appetites and we are not fond of suppressing them. But if we cannot even say no to one bowl of macaroni and cheese, how will we be able to say no when something with serious stakes arises? Fasting is good training, reminding our minds, spirits and bodies that God is our real sustenance. Fasting is also a way to keep our hearts longing for Jesus. Jesus said in Mark 2:20 that, "The time will come when the bridegroom will be taken from them, and on that day they will fast." Fasting is a way to express our hunger and longing for the bridegroom, Jesus, to return for His bride, the Church.

Another important spiritual discipline is *study*, and by this I mean reading the Bible and really thinking about what we have read. Study is pouring over the Word of God and meditating upon it, so its words can sink in and bring life and healing and wisdom.

Again, start small and work your way up. It is like going to the gym. No one can lift the heaviest weights on the first day, but with daily discipline and stretching and exercise, we will soon find ourselves doing more than we ever thought we could. Reading and studying are the same way.

One of the best things we can do is to stretch our minds and really think about the Lord on a regular basis; daily, if possible. The Bible should be the mainstay of our devotional life, but also important are great Christian books. We like to call them "Old Dead Guys and Gals," or ODG's. Many of the men and women who have walked before us have lived and learned such tremendous truths about God and His kingdom; it is good for our hearts and minds to listen to them in order to keep ourselves searching and growing, and keep our hearts full of wonder at the sheer magnitude of God and His character. The eternal story that all of us get to be a part of is so much more immense than any of us can see from our limited perspective. It is encouraging and sustaining to keep our eyes focused on God's big picture.

The Outward Disciplines: Simplicity, Solitude, Submission, Service
These are the practices we have that other people can see. They, too, are a part of our spiritual workout regimen as a Christian, and the ones that everyone else in the world can plainly see in us. These are the practices that make us different, and that show the world what it looks like to walk with God.

First is *simplicity*. In a world so insanely obsessed with more, newer, better, faster and shinier, simplicity makes a great impact. Living simply means choosing to not jump into the storage facility culture that surrounds us. It means not having more than I need for myself, so that I always have plenty to share with my neighbor. It means buying a used car and taking the extra money I would have spent on a new one and using it to support a missionary. It means choosing mission over money, choosing to live so I can make an impact on the world for Jesus and not just where I can get the fattest paycheck. Simplicity is setting boundaries for myself, my money and my time, using them all for God's purposes and not for my own accumulation of wealth and power.

Next is *solitude*. There are two kinds of people in the world: those who love to be around people all the time, and those who love not to be around people all the time. This discipline is for all of us, but mainly for the "people" people. Solitude is needing nothing but God. In a day where it is difficult to get away from electronic things and constant noise, we must seek solitude and incorporate it into our schedules. It is waiting in the presence of the Lord. It is being still and just knowing that He is God. It is taking a break from the pressure for social media likes, from the constant need of affirmation from others, and from noise and chatter and conversation to rest quietly in God.

Third is *submission*, and this is such an important discipline to practice. The world tells us that the goal is to be on top, that we need to push and climb until we get there. God tells us that to be a leader means to be a servant, that the top is actually the bottom. We practice submission to God in obeying His commands, and we practice submission to one another by putting others' needs higher than our own. We also practice submission by refusing to fall into the trap that "my way" is always the right way. We submit to one another by honoring each other and in seeing that God is working in each one of us. It is healthy to bow and let others lead. It is healthy not to always be the boss, but the servant.

Finally in this section of outward disciplines is *service*. This is how Christians can shine in a community. Where do hospitals come from? Orphanages, schools, prison ministries, soup kitchens? These are all outreaches of the Christian community throughout the ages. Jesus came to heal the sick, bind up the broken, care for the widow and orphan, and help prisoners, and we are to act just like Him. Service is showing the people all around us that God loves them and so do we. It is one thing to preach sermons—and we should—but it is another thing to live out the things we preach on a regular basis. The words we say mean so much more to people when they are backed up by selfless service to others.

The Corporate Disciplines:
Confession. Worship, Guidance, Celebration

These last four spiritual disciplines are the ones we practice together. They are a part of our spiritual workout, and help make us strong and keep us strong.

We have just spent a lot of time in southern Colorado/northern New Mexico, and one of the most beautiful sights in that region are the aspen trees. They are glorious! I never realized, but they are all connected as a single organism. What happens to one tree affects all of the others. When one tree gets something helpful, it is shared with all of the rest. This is a beautiful picture of Christianity! We are all connected and we can help each other. These corporate disciplines are what keep us healthy and thriving.

We practice things like *confession*, which is admitting our weaknesses and failures to God and one another. We are not playing a game here. Being honest with each another can help us all live healthier and stronger lives. Confession allows for forgiveness, which is a powerful thing. Being open with each other on a regular basis makes us want to live rightly, and that accountability is helpful to all of us.

We *worship together*, not forsaking meeting together regularly (Heb. 10:25). Yes, we can walk with God alone, but we are not called to. There is power when two or three of us gather together. Our corporate worship is a strong testimony to unbelievers we might bring with us. As we turn our attention and adoration together towards God, our faith is strengthened.

Seeking *guidance* is a wonderful discipline. How many disasters in relationship, finance, business and child rearing could be avoided if we just sought godly counsel beforehand? One of the most beautiful things about being a Christian is that we are not alone. We have the presence of God always with us, and the fellowship and wisdom of all our brothers and sisters, too. Practicing the discipline of seeking guidance regularly builds a healthy life.

Finally is the discipline of *celebration*. I love the way Foster chooses to end the study of disciplines with this. Celebration is the joy that comes from knowing we have been saved and set free by Jesus, and have lived our lives for His kingdom. It is likened to the difference between a piano player at the beginning of his studies (which is surely frustrating and difficult as his fingers learn to navigate the keyboard rightly) and that same player as he is mastering the piece. The one who has mastered the piece can actually feel the joy and strength in the music. It is this joy and the strength it brings that keeps us moving forward; it is knowing what is coming that helps us stay focused and full of joy and peace.

This is celebration of Christians everywhere. We learn, together, to walk with God and know Him, and we celebrate, together, in the joy that comes from fellowshipping with God. We are not mindless, joyless robots; we are people who live daily in the freedom of our salvation. Walking with God is not a drudgery or a chore. Rather, it is a delight; a daily celebration of the faithfulness and goodness of the God we love and trust. Even better, it is an endless celebration as we spend eternity together in heaven.

Application

Which of these twelve areas of spiritual disciplines most stirred you as you read this chapter? Take time to reflect on how you could incorporate these disciplines into your life. Start with the one or two that intrigued you most as you read, and make a conscious effort to practice these several times throughout the next season.

Consider using the Purposes and Goals exercise to make solid plans for adding new disciplines to your spiritual workout regimen. Even better, get together with a small group of friends and plan to practice together. I encourage you to read *Celebration of Discipline* to better understand each practice.

KINGDOM MINDED

NINE

Bringing Order to Disorder in the Mind, Body and Spirit

Most of us, especially if we are born again as adults, begin our Christian walk with great disorder of the mind, body and spirit. Our "room" is a huge mess. We do not even know how much we do not know. Statistics tell us that most Christians have never read the entire Bible, so we can be sure that most people who were not raised as Christians have never read the Bible. Without reading the Word and without the conviction of the Holy Spirit that all Christians experience, how can someone know what truth is, or what the standard of holiness is, or how people ought to live? Most people just walk around with the sense that life is hard and often terrible. They realize life is not supposed to be this way, but they have no idea how to find peace.

Adding to this is the reality that the enemy has done a very good job of convincing people—especially people who have influence in education and entertainment—that there is no connection between what happens in the body and what happens in the mind and spirit. They say you can do whatever you want, whenever you want, to or with whomever you want and it does not matter at all. This is a lie as old as the Fall itself, and we must fight against it, still. People are lured to their eternal deaths with the idea that what they do does not matter.

Regardless what kind of home we grew up in, what kind of experiences we have had, what kind of attitudes and beliefs we have formed, every person who has been born again of the Spirit of God has to make the journey from selfish to godly. In an earlier chapter, we looked at the difference between the kingdom of darkness, everyone's starting place, and the kingdom of light, our home for now and eternity as followers of Jesus. Spiritual disciplines are the building blocks God uses to restore order in our lives, and to conform us into the image of Christ, choice by choice, obedience by obedience.

One of the major beliefs in Christianity is that God is not just one Person; rather, He is three in one. He is the Father, the Son and the Holy Spirit. This is referred to as the Trinity. Just as God is three Persons in one, we are also three parts in one. We are made in His image, after all. We are a spirit, created by God to live forever. We have a mind, also often called a heart or soul, and can think and feel and make choices. We are born and live in a body that God knit together in a mother's womb. This body houses our spirit and mind until death takes us out of that body. The body we live in now is the one piece of us that changes with death (1 Cor. 15: 35-58). The rest of us will continue to live forever in either heaven or hell. These three parts work together to make us who we are now. We cannot separate the three; they work together, for good or for ill.

This means that to bring discipline into our lives, we must address the disorder in all three parts of ourselves: the mind, body and spirit. They are so inextricably connected that either all are healthy and ordered, or they are not. Like the aspen trees, everything that happens to one part of the self affects the others. There is so much that could be said about each of these, so let's take just a glimpse of what to be aware of in this current age.

The Mind: What I Think

Minds are amazing things. Our thoughts are active every waking moment, and then they keep on spinning all night long in our dreams. How interesting that the mind never shuts off! There is a part of our mind that facilitates this unconscious, sleep-time-thinking, and it is a mystery and a miracle.

Then there are parts of our physical brains that house the control panels for all of our bodily functions, and these parts are so incredibly efficient that we never have to consciously tap into that piece of our mind.

The part of the mind for this discussion is the conscious, "thinking-and-choosing" piece of the mind. We have the capacity to have total control over this part of ourselves. The problem comes when we do not guard our mind or pay attention to what is going into it. We have all been born at a time of sensory and information overload. Two thousand years ago, even two hundred years ago, it would have been almost totally impossible to be taking in information and stimulation all day, every day, like a person can in this era. Before electricity, there was much more time to just "be." Now, we very likely can stay up all night reading or watching movies or playing video games, with bright lights mimicking daytime. We can have music pouring into our ears through our personal headsets all day, every day. We can watch anything we want on television or a computer screen whenever we want. We really can spend all day, every day doing innocuous things online like posting kitten pictures, or staying glued to much more destructive things.

This endless supply of ready-made images for the mind is quite dangerous. Studies show these actually are making all of us dumber, not wiser. How sad it would be for all of us if some of the greatest thinkers, creators and doers of the past were as plugged in as we are. Would William Wilberforce and his peers have succeeded in bringing down the slave trade like they did, or would they have been satisfied at being really good at video games and making clever social media posts?

We are what we think. When we spend all day taking in carefully packaged images (by someone with an agenda), we are putting our minds at risk for chaos and disorder. We are letting our minds dwell on what someone else wants us to think. Many times it is a carefully packaged lie, but the more we look at it and listen to it, the more our minds will store that information as truth and normality. If something does not line up with what we know to be true, do not spend time watching or listening to that thing. Lies believed in the mind cause chaos and disorder in the spirit, as well.

Some of us were absolutely steeped in the thinking of the world when we became Christians. We never considered whether what we were watching, reading, listening to, or being taught was actual truth or whether it was a lie. We never once worried whether the things we thought about were real or false. We rolled along with everyone else, and thought the way everyone else thought. But when the veil was removed, we were able to see that what had been sold to us as truth was actually a lie. Now we feel the disorder of having old thoughts and beliefs that do not line up with what the Word of God says is truth.

The great news is that the Bible teaches we can control our minds. We can absolutely control what we think. When those thoughts and images from the old way of life pass through our brains, we can do what 2 Corinthians 10:5 instructs: "Demolish arguments and every pretension that sets itself up against the knowledge of God, and we take captive every thought to make it obedient to Christ." This language is appropriately violent and aggressive. When something false floats through, we can attack it and replace it with what is true. We no longer dwell on lies or sit staring mindlessly at a screen; we actively control our thought life.

We control what gets put into our minds by putting in good things, like, what makes up a healthy devotional life, and by no longer putting in or dwelling on bad or numbing things that frustrate the order God is restoring to our minds.

The Body: What I Do

There is such dignity in realizing that my body and life are not just some strange happenstance of evolution. I am not an accident, and neither are you. No one is. God made each of us on purpose and with purpose. (Really knowing and understanding this would completely eliminate racism, classism and feelings of uselessness.) We know that our bodies are not going to last forever, but we also know that while we are in them, we must care for them.

1 Corinthians 6: 19-20 tells us, "Do you not know that your bodies are temples of the Holy Spirit, who is in you, whom you have received from God? You are not your own; you were bought at a price. Therefore honor God with your bodies."

For illustration, we can think of our bodies as a car. Brand new, a car is clean and shiny, and all we have to do is put in gas, turn the key, and go. It will keep on running just fine for quite a long time. We can even put in cheap gas, never wash it, and get away with not changing the oil or the tires. Eventually, however, the day comes when the car cannot go on anymore. Rust might overrun the entire undercarriage; the engine might get gummed up and seize; and the tires might explode while we are driving down the interstate. We can ignore our car and abuse it, but we will have to pay for our neglect at some point.

Our bodies are just the same. We can get away with so much when we are young, but as we do, we develop really poor habits that last a lifetime. It truly is important to take care of our bodies, or they will not last very long or very well. Many illnesses that people suffer in life are not mysteries; they are caused by lack of care and by consistently ignoring practices of good health. This involves all the things we vaguely know are important, like eating proper amounts of healthy food, getting consistent good sleep, abstaining from harmful substances, and exercising regularly. Like everything else, good habits go the distance here. Keeping healthy boundaries and practices will help our bodies last as long as they need to without causing our loved ones to watch us suffer because of a lifetime of poor habits.

The other piece we must be consider here is the idea that our body is a holy temple. This age tells us that illicit sex is no big deal. People engage in casual hook-ups with people they barely even know.

But look around. Is every one of these people really happy and content? Of course not! Anxiety, confusion and hopelessness are off the charts. We are supposed to believe that the celebrities who go from one partner to another, even getting married to one now and then until someone better comes along, have a perfect life and that such behavior is perfectly normal and even admirable. Are we supposed to pretend there is no connection when those same celebrities go in and out of rehab every other year, and sometimes take their own lives? And what about the mental and spiritual health of their children? We cannot lie to ourselves that living entirely to satisfy every desire of our flesh is healthy or okay.

Men and women were not created to have sexual relationships with anyone and everyone. The biblical standard is one man and one woman, committed for life. There are stories in the Bible about people who did not follow God's model and incurred heartache, trouble and overall calamity for everyone involved.

When we marry and join together with our spouse, something spiritual happens: We become one flesh (Mark 10: 6-9.). There is an incredibly real and powerful bond that occurs when two hearts are knit together in love and unity. Such a bond creates a safe place for the rearing of our children. When we sleep around, we give pieces of our hearts away to people who have no intention of staying in commitment, which is chaotic and causes real issues of loss and abandonment.

In our years of campus ministry, we have talked with hundreds of students who had been promiscuous before becoming Christians. The common realization is that there is no such thing as casual sex. All sex outside marriage has a spiritual component—it is not just a function of the body, no matter how much anyone wants that to be true.

We cannot use our bodies to create disorder in our minds and spirits. 1 Corinthians 6:18-20 instructs us to:

> Flee from sexual immorality. All other sins a man commits are outside his body, but he who sins sexually sins against his own body. Do you not know that your body is a temple of the Holy Spirit, who is in you, whom you have received from God? You are not your own; you were bought at a price. Therefore honor God with your body.

The Spirit: What I Worship

We are made in God's image, so we are spirit like He is. We were created also to worship, which means to turn our full attention to and give our lives to God. Obviously, many people have not yet come to know God, but that does not mean their spirits are not worshipping something. None of us can worship nothing; our spirits must worship something. If not God it could be any number of things we worship: power, money, sex, a person, an idea, a false god—anything. Whatever we turn our full attention to, whatever our life revolves around, that is what we worship. It is an activity of the spirit which almost always also involves both the body and the mind. Every part of us is involved in our worship of whatever we have fixed our gaze upon.

This is a good place to address a topic that must be mentioned: pornography. This is a terrifying worship of sex that is stealing millions of spirits, minds and bodies all across the globe. Millennials (and those even younger) have a challenge that no other age bracket in the history of the world has had to face. Pornography is not new, but it has always been much harder to access. Further, in the past, pornography was also accompanied by an appropriate level of shame. Not anymore. These days, from the time we are old enough to turn on a screen, we have had the opportunity to tune into anything, anytime.

Worse than that, porn has become so normalized to this generation that the shame of viewing and making pornography is almost totally gone. It is not uncommon at all to hear about ten-year-olds sending each other lewd pictures on their phones. And, as many know, the diminishing thrill is chased by ever stronger and more dangerous images.

As with any other addiction, an addiction to pornography affects not only us, but everyone around us. If we are addicted to pornography, we are numb to reality and normalcy. If we are addicted to pornography, we have warped our mind's ability to think clearly. It negatively affects all of our relationships.

Wicked people in the pornography industry have stolen our innocence and ability to think rightly about ourselves, each other and healthy sexuality. Ruining our minds has made them very rich. They have convinced us that what we watch in the privacy of our own rooms has no impact on anyone else. They have destroyed our ability to have healthy marriages. They have hurt innumerable children and young people all over the world in making images to give us just one more thrill. It is a lie that pornography does not hurt anyone; it destroys real people, including everyone addicted to it.

This is exactly what the prince of the kingdom of darkness loves. He wants nothing more than to destroy God's sons and daughters because he hates God so much. God made each of us male or female, and created our bodies in such a compatible way that sex is a natural and wonderful thing within the safe confines of a committed marriage. This healthy relationship produces children, a miracle. It is God's way of bringing babies into the world.

Do you see how pornography and the culture of sex worship robs all that? It takes away the safety and commitment. It takes away the fact that sex is for creating children. It introduces all kinds of repulsive and unnatural ideas which become normalized the more one watches.

Instead of being the avenue for literal fruitfulness in the begetting of children, sex becomes the selfish chasing of a feeling which lasts for just a moment and is never as satisfying as hoped. Instead of sex being a part of mature adulthood, creating children that we must selflessly care for and nurture as mothers and fathers, sex becomes a creepy ritual of worship that makes people predators—seeking whom they can devour. Sexual pursuit becomes the hunt of a predator for a victim.

I will never forget the first time I heard a particular missionary to India speak. He and his family had spent decades working to share the love and hope of Jesus in some of the darkest places on earth. This missionary family had a ministry that went right into the brothels of the Indian slums to help bring people out of that horrible life. He showed us pictures of the women they ministered to who were essentially sex slaves, owned by wicked people who sold them by the half hour to locals and tourists alike. These young women looked so used—because they were.

Then he showed us pictures of the children born to these women, little boys and girls who might never know a life away from such evil, and who are often sold into the sex trade themselves when they are still very young. I used every single napkin on the dinner table that night (and maybe even the tablecloth) as I wept uncontrollably. I had never made the connection in my mind with how all of the tentacles of sex worship are connected: movies and shows that make porn seem funny and normal, porn sites with mild pictures, hardcore porn, the global sex trade, human trafficking. It is all connected and it is destroying real lives all over the world.

I want to tell you today that there is hope yet. In Romans 12: 1-2, Paul instructs us, "Therefore, I urge you, brothers and sisters, in view of God's mercy, to offer your bodies as a living sacrifice, holy and pleasing to God—this is your true and proper worship. Do not conform to the pattern of this world, but be transformed by the renewing of your mind." God can renew your mind and spirit. God can remake the pathways in your brain that have been warped by a porn addiction. He can roll over them like a steam roller and replace awful images with pure, clean thoughts.

If your life is gripped by this dragon of pornography, you must take serious and severe action to change your habits and thoughts. Jesus said in Matthew 5:27-30:

> You have heard that it was said, "You shall not commit adultery." But I tell you that anyone who looks at a woman lustfully has already committed adultery with her in his heart. If your right eye causes you to stumble, gouge it out and throw it away. It is better for you to lose one part of your body than for your whole body to be thrown into hell. And if your right hand causes you to stumble, cut it off and throw it away. It is better for you to lose one part of your body than for your whole body to go into hell.

Jesus knew what kind of trouble you might find yourself in. The internet was far in the future at that point, but Jesus has always known the weakness of mankind and the wicked propensity of our sinful nature. He is saying here that we cannot believe the lie that something we do in our mind, alone in our room, is not hurting anyone. We cannot disconnect the mind, body and spirit. What happens in one part affects all the rest. Jesus is telling us that if something like sex worship is hurting us and binding us, we have to act really drastically to stop it. It is that terribly dangerous.

What should a person do who is addicted to pornography? First, be honest with yourself and someone you can trust that you have a serious problem. Be honest! Not just once, but forever. Get it all out in the open. Ask God for forgiveness of this sin, then repent—turn around and go the other way from your old patterns. Make a real plan to change your behavior.

This is not going to be easy, and I will tell you right now that you are a fool if you think you can trust yourself with the internet right at first. If your entire generation needs to get rid of your smartphones and computers and go back to paper Day Planners, pens, notebooks, typewriters, encyclopedias and landline phones, so be it. I volunteer to join with you in solidarity. We cannot let you and your children be killed by this plague. Drastic action is required to become free of this deadly snare.

Turn to Jesus, and turn your worship to Him. Maybe you need to take a retreat to somewhere with no access, somewhere you can break the grip of this habit, and breathe the free air for the first time in a long time. Ask God to wash your mind and renew your thoughts and purity. Be persistent in prayer. Fill your mind and thoughts with beautiful things, with the Bible, with good books about the greatness of God and His character. Do this daily, frequently, until you have established new and godly habits, and then work hard to keep those good habits. The cross was not too weak to defeat the sin of pornography. The blood of Jesus is sufficient, and He has overcome the world. Let God transform you, and know that He will be with you every step of the way.

Application

This chapter has dealt with some very heavy and serious issues. Please take the time to evaluate and treat seriously the things you focus your mind, body and spirit upon. I lovingly challenge you to unplug from the internet for a day, a week or even a month, starting today. Let the love of God wash, renew and transform you.

TEN

A Life that Matters

Do you believe anybody can change the world? Do you think it is even possible? Do you think it has ever happened before?

I mean, yes, we all know and believe that Jesus changed the world. But what about His people; can an ordinary Christian change the world?

Let me introduce you to a group of people you might never have heard of that did just that.

First, a little background to remind us of some British history. England went back and forth between being Catholic and Protestant for about a hundred years after the Reformation, and sometimes things got violent. For a brief time in the 1630s, there was a Civil War in England. People actually killed the king and were ruled by a Protectorate. When the monarchy was restored twenty years later in 1660, the new king (who happened to be the son of the murdered king) wanted very little to do with an active Christianity.

By the early 1700s, England was really tired of the back and forth fight of "Are we Protestant or Catholic?" People wanted the debate to end so they could get on with their lives.

Not surprisingly, then, it did not take long for morality to tank. English society got really, really bad. We can make a good argument that it was even worse than our own society is today. In the 1730s, the infant mortality rate was seventy-five percent. The favorite public sports were dog-fighting and bull-baiting; animals were killed in awful, torturous ways for fun and sport. One out of every five women was a prostitute. Alcoholism was rampant; people were afraid to drink the water because of the plague, so they drank gin instead and gave it to their kids!

By law, poor people were not allowed to learn to read or write; the government was afraid that if they were educated, there would be revolution. Society was horrible, without hope. This was a nation that called itself Christian, but forgot to act like it.

Then, a couple of brothers named John and Charles Wesley came along. They actually had read the Bible and got very serious about living out their faith. They got very serious about holiness, about reading and knowing the Scriptures and praying, about sharing their faith with people who did not know God, and about living life in community with other believers. Slowly, the tide actually began to turn as they shared the true good news.

By the time the Wesleys were elderly in the late 1700s, thousands and thousands of people in England and America had been influenced by their teachings and methods. It is a particular grouping of these people that I want to introduce us to.

They were various individuals who believed Jesus was real, and His power could change one person's heart as well as the heart of a city, a nation and the whole world. They were called by God to take part in doing just that. They were politicians, writers, preachers, actors, singers, teachers, bankers and artisans who dared to believe that real Christianity could be lived out. They all had huge dreams individually, dreams to make a real difference. God had empowered each of these people with incredible creativity and skill in their respective fields.

Meet Hannah More, a best-selling author, also a teacher by trade (yes, both were unusual for a woman at that time), who believed all children should be able to read. She had the incredible idea to invite the children of her village to church on Sundays, the only day the children did not have to work, and then invite them to stay for school all day. She gave them a meal and reading lessons.

Meet Henry Thornton. He was a banker and economist, and was quite wealthy. Before he married, he gave eighty percent of his income away to help the poor and spread the gospel. After he married, it was about fifty percent, which is still incredibly and challengingly generous.

Meet William Wilberforce, a member of Parliament by age twenty-five. He had hundreds of good ideas to improve society. He started the Society for the Prevention of Cruelty to Animals, so people could be informed to treat animals kindly and not cruelly, as was the fashion. He wrote a best-selling book called *A Practical View of the Prevailing Religious System of Professed Christians in the Higher and Middle Classes in this Country Contrasted with Real Christianity*, which is a great title. He also had a personal conviction and agenda that the slave trade must end.

In 1790, Henry Thornton bought a house in a town some five miles outside of London called Clapham. Within a few short years, Thornton, Wilberforce, More and about thirty others had bought or built homes around this first house so they could live in proximity to, and in community with, one another, to pool their talents, ideas and resources, and get serious about changing the world. They never gave themselves a name, but people noticed them and their absolutely enormous influence and called them the Clapham Sect.

So, when William Wilberforce's first bill to abolish the slave trade was defeated in 1791 (when he was only thirty-two!) the Clapham bunch decided to band together to change the earth.

KINGDOM MINDED

Hannah More wrote books and plays about the evils of slavery and about the dignity of every man, woman and child.

The poets wrote beautiful poems; the singers sang catchy, memorable songs about the evil of the slave trade; the actors staged plays.

The potters crafted gorgeous vases and plates and porcelain brooches with the image of a slave and the caption, "Am I not a man?" which were best-sellers. Ever hear of Josiah Wedgewood, famous for Wedgewood pottery? He did that.

The painters made posters depicting the evils of the slave trade and sold them to shopkeepers for their windows.

Olaudah Equiano, a freed slave who had been blessed to learn to read in captivity, wrote his life story, revealing the horror of slavery from the inside. It was a runaway best seller.

The politicians worked together tirelessly to get the votes.

Essentially, they commandeered popular culture with anti-slavery sentiment. And they pooled their own money together to pay for all this.

It took thirty years of organized effort, but we know today that legitimized slavery is a thing of the past. In 1826, the slave trade was abolished in the British Empire and these were the people who made it happen—ordinary Christians who dared to live their Christianity and do extraordinary things.

Is taking down the slave trade, an ancient, wicked practice, not enough for you?

They started and financed the missions movement and effort into India.

They reversed the rampant alcoholism problem.

They started Sunday schools and regular schools and made the literacy rate go through the roof.

They reformed prisons.

They started orphanages.

They organized homes and shelters for the poor.

They helped return dignity to women.

They fought for better conditions for workers.

They brought back decency to popular music, literature and the stage.

They were a passionate few who lived in community on purpose, and changed the entire Western World.

Now, what about you and me? Too many of us are choosing money over mission. We put out our applications and go wherever we can get the fattest paycheck. Often, we go there alone, without any friends or family around to be a healthy and supportive community, and then we wonder why we are so discouraged and alone. Our lives become a dull routine of clocking in and clocking out, stirring very little creativity in our hearts and minds and having very little impact on our neighborhoods.

What if we made disciplined choices to choose mission over money, and decided to live in proximity to and in community with one another, to pool our talents, ideas and resources, and get serious about changing the world? What could our generation accomplish if we who seek to follow Jesus banded together like the Clapham Sect chose to do?

It actually says in Genesis 11 that if we work together, there is nothing we cannot do. How powerful it could be if we all took our faith seriously and determined in our hearts to make our lives count for eternity! The social justice issues that frustrate so many would be naturally eliminated if the good news of Jesus were really proclaimed again. The poor would be cared for, the overlooked would be welcomed and encouraged, the broken and confused would be set free, and the evil practices of greedy, selfish people would be eliminated.

Not only could our own communities be transformed, but we could band together to send missionaries to the ends of the earth. There are millions of people who have still never heard the gospel, and we can no longer hide behind the excuse that it is impossible to get there; the world is more connected than ever. The reason so many have never heard about Jesus is because we do not give enough money or prayer support to send those who are willing to go, nor will most of us go ourselves. We could be the generation who finishes the task of letting the whole world know about the saving power of Jesus, if we just will.

History tells us that a passionate few, living in community and on purpose, can change truly the world.

Will we accept the challenge in our generation?

*The facts and statistics in this chapter are all drawn from three books I love and highly recommend to you:

England Before and After Wesley by J. Wesley Bready
Fierce Convictions: The Extraordinary Life of Hannah More—Poet, Reformer, Abolitionist by Karen Swallow Prior
7 Women: And the Secret of Their Greatness by Eric Metaxas

Application

A Prayer of Willingness:
Lord God, I offer myself, my talent and my life to You. I ask that You take all of this, and unite me with a community of like-minded brothers and sisters. Help us to work together to bring real hope and change into the world. Help us to be generous, creative, inspired, encouraging and useful for Your glory on the earth. Amen.

Now, call the friends God has put on your heart and begin to dream together.

KINGDOM MINDED

ELEVEN

The City on a Hill

By this everyone will know that you are My disciples, if you love one another.
John 13:35

It is very likely you have been walking with God long enough to realize that things are not always quite like you expected and Christianity is not easy. It is easy enough to understand, but really difficult to actually live.

Eli and I had two very different childhoods with respect to church. I was the child who grew up there: always in Sunday School, Vacation Bible School, youth group, Sunday morning worship services, all of it. Eli had very little church experience before college. Please notice that both of us were equally lost when we encountered Jesus. He was lost outside the church walls and I was lost inside them. Neither of us had a real relationship with Jesus, which is what being a Christian is all about.

When we began hanging around a Chi Alpha group at the University of the Pacific, Eli remembers being so struck by how kind everyone was. They said really nice things to each other, and actually seemed to truly care about how we were doing. How different! Most people love to make fun of each other and put each other down in painful ways. Somehow this is an accepted practice in society, as long as you are sure to add, "Just joking!" One guy told Eli he really liked his shirt, and Eli kept waiting for the rude punchline, but it never came because that Christian meant just what he said. These Christians loved and honored each other, and it was striking.

When we gave our hearts to Jesus and were born again, it seemed to me as if the whole world was sunshine and roses. There is hope and joy and peace when you know the Lord, and it felt great to experience these and be around many others who had also experienced them.

Then, a year or two later, I had the sad realization that there were really grumpy and mean people inside the church, too. It was so disheartening to me. This is the very thing that makes it harder than it should be for people to stay in the faith. It is such a turn off when Christians are selfish and mean and rude, just like everyone else. There are a few lessons here that would take too much time to really flesh out, but suffice it to say that we cannot judge anyone; only God can do that. And, as Christians, we need to take very seriously the picture of Jesus that we are painting to each other and those outside the church.

What does it mean to love? Jesus said in John 13 that others will know we follow Him by our love for one another. This means that when we love each other, it will be noticeable and impactful. But, oftentimes, we think loving each other is difficult. We have the mistaken idea that love is a feeling, that I can only love someone if they make me feel happy or content, or some other feeling.

This is simply not true. Love is not a feeling, it is a choice, and the sooner we all get a hold of this truth, the better. Love is a choice for the highest good of God and His kingdom, every single time. I choose to love my family, my friends, my church and my community, and I do so because that is exactly what God does every day without fail. When I make a choice to love and honor them no matter how they treat me or how they make me feel, it impacts them deeply.

What does it mean to honor someone? To honor something means to add or give value, and to place weight upon it. There are several characteristics that can make something valuable, things like beauty, or rarity, or strength. This is called an intrinsic value. For example, diamonds are valuable because they have all of those things. People have an intrinsic value, as well, simply because they are made in the glorious image of God. We honor every person's God-given worth, dignity and value, and when we do this they begin to see, often for the first time in their lives, that they have purpose, dignity, and a reason for being alive.

Every single person we meet has a different facet of God represented in his or her life, and it is only when we are all together that we get a full representation of God. This is such a big thing. Jesus died for each of us. We are all precious to Him and we should treat one another accordingly.

Do we really mean what we say when we say we would do anything for Jesus? Then we will love our neighbor as He loves them. We will stop letting every single thought, snarky remark, and bad mood spill out all over our families and the ones dearest to us. We will choose to treat people rightly and to speak to them and treat them as God does. We will stop being so hyper-critical of each other. Anyone can see what's wrong with you or with me, but we need to be people who see what's right in each other and the people we encounter every day.

This is precisely how we can engage and win people who do not know Jesus—by becoming the best friends they have ever known. We love and honor them, and eventually earn their trust and the right to speak into their lives. We have to remember that love and laughter plow hard hearts. Even the rockiest and stoniest hearts cannot long ignore the power of true love and honor and selflessness. This is the story of the *Beauty and the Beast* and *The Velveteen Rabbit*. If you have never read these children's classics, you should. True love helps people become real and who God created them to be.

A friend of ours was once making a point to hang out with people on campus who were outside of her usual social circles so she might find an opportunity to introduce them to Jesus. She found herself making friends with the leader of a pretty radical progressive group. They spent time together and eventually really talked about real-life things, becoming friends.

It was a great joy for our friend to see a social media conversation between her new friend and the other members of her group. The girl posted, "I am surprised by how nice [she] is. I think maybe I have been wrong about Christians."

Her friend replied, "Watch out! That is how they get you!" We all enjoyed that very much.

God draws us to Himself with His very kindness, and we should do the same for others (Rom. 2:4). We hear it over and over again, "I have never been treated that way; I have never been loved like that; I didn't know relationships like this really existed." In fact, this is my story, too! When this happens to any of us, we can't wait to pass it on to others. Real love changes lives.

Practically speaking, what does loving and honoring someone look like? There are many things we can do.

Never let someone be the awkward person standing by themselves, even if she acts awkwardly.

Ask him questions.

Let him be the expert about whatever it is he loves. Let him teach you something.

Look for the good and honorable in someone, and praise it. "I love how you..." "I really admire...."

Speak well about her in front of others and behind her back. Help everyone to love and think highly of one another.

Totally and mercilessly eliminate all negative talk and comments, even those in jest.

Have a furious commitment to unselfishness; do and talk about things he loves that otherwise you would not care less about.

Serve people. Do kind and helpful things for others.

Pray for them, not just in theory, but in practice, and often. This is the best thing we can do for people, but most of us terribly neglect prayer. We worry, but we do not pray. Lift them up before God. You might be the only person on earth who is praying for that particular individual.

We are not living this way and honoring people just to boost our group's numbers, or to look cool or holy in front of everyone else, but because Jesus counted them as worthy of His life, so we do, too. Francis Schaeffer said there are no little people and no little places. Every man, woman and child really does bear God's image and is worthy of our honor.

Now let's talk about the fact that the way we interact with each other either confirms and enhances or totally negates our witness to those around us. It is literally repulsive when we act horribly and selfishly to each other; it repels people from wanting to know us and our God. That is a terrible reflection of God's character. When we live in disunity, it robs our entire Christian community of the blessing that God breathes on people of unity (Ps. 133.) We know and believe and have seen that evil has power, but do we know and believe that we, through God, can have power, too? There is true spiritual power when Christians live together in unity of heart—power to draw others to the grace and forgiveness of Christ.

Unity is powerful. Communist theorists got some points right, which is why those ideas are perpetually appealing to so many people. But they missed the mark because without God in their system, the people at the top invariably become corrupted by the lure of power. Unity does not mean we are all exactly the same: nameless, faceless members of the masses. Unity means I know where I stand in God's eyes and I know where you stand, too. Unity means true unselfishness: My time is yours and my prayers are yours, and if you are in need of something I have, you are welcome to it.

In our time as university campus pastors, we have seen dozens of car titles change hands when someone was in need. We have seen small groups band together to help someone pay tuition so they could graduate. We have seen people give away watches and jackets and shoes—the list goes on and on.

Unity also means commitment; we are totally committed to one another "'til death do us part." We must have a fierce and unending love for one another. Nothing you can do or say will make me stop loving you and hoping the best for you. This kind of unity makes our community strong and thriving; it makes our fellowship something others want to be a part of.

Of course, it is good for a child to know his parents love him, but it is just as important for him to know that Mom and Dad love each other and are not going anywhere. People of all ages long for safety and security, for a safe place to grow and thrive. Our love for one another becomes a magnet to the lost. Through our love for Christ and each another, we become the city on a hill, shining like a beacon of hope for everyone.

God Himself loves each of us with the most powerful love, and He teaches us to love one another. He talks to us, deals with us, challenges us, and reminds us to be kind and humble and put others ahead of ourselves.

We must never let our guard down here. We often do, and this is a place the enemy attacks and defeats us. He gets an evil thrill out of dividing us. We can be very good at putting on a veneer of love and trust and honor for one another while still allowing negative and even wicked thoughts to mill around in our spirits and even come out of our mouths.

Proverbs 6 says that one of the things God hates is a person who stirs up conflict in the community. This is terrifying. We cannot cause division and dissention in our communities. Satan is called "the accuser of the brethren" (Rev. 12:10, KJV). Do we really want to help him do his job? Certainly not! We want to love, honor and trust one another, above all else.

One of the most familiar verses in the Bible is John 3:16, which says, "For God so loved the world that He gave His one and only Son, that whoever believes in Him shall not perish but have eternal life."

In God's great patience, His plan to reach every person on earth with this love is for His people to generously share the Good News. We can, should and will have fellowship that is better, deeper and richer than anything this world has ever seen.

When we practice the disciplines of honoring and loving each other, our communities become like a delicious soup: Together, we are something rich and nourishing and flavorful that flows out onto the people around us. Together we can impact the world in a greater way and represent God more accurately and completely than we can alone.

Application

Turn in your Bible to 1 Corinthians 13 and read the entire chapter out loud a time or two.

Now, read it through out loud again, but when you get to verses 4-7, replace the word "love" with your first name. Let the Holy Spirit gently nudge and challenge you on the places you need it. Be honest with yourself and with the Lord. "Am I patient? Am I kind?" Continue through the chapter with an open heart and with open ears.

Pray and ask God to change your heart, tame your tongue, and give you real love for your brothers and sisters.

TWELVE

There is More

"Do not leave Jerusalem, but wait for the gift My Father promised, which you have heard Me speak about. For John baptized with water, but in a few days you will be baptized with the Holy Spirit." Acts 1:4-5

It is safe to say that just about everyone loves to receive gifts. It is a special feeling to realize that someone has been thinking fondly of you, enough to go out of their way to buy and present you with something special. What is even more amazing is when the person giving the gift really knows you and knows exactly what will make you happiest.

In our family, many are very kind and generous, but the person with the greatest measure of this talent is my sister. When boxes or envelopes arrive from her particular address, everyone gets very excited. She is good! We cannot figure out how she does it, but she always knows the perfect gift. And she is exceptionally generous, so she always gets the kind of luxurious thing you would never buy for yourself.

What if God were to give you a present? What might it be? His resources are endless and He is the very definition of generosity. He knows us better than we know ourselves, and knows exactly what we need. Just like the expectant thrill when packages arrive from my sister, it is a sure thing that a present from God will be the best present ever.

How interesting it is that Jesus instructs His followers to wait for the gift the Father promised. I am sure they felt ready to get out there and tell everyone about what they had seen—the Messiah truly had come! But Jesus said, "Wait for the gift." And how interesting it is that this makes so many of us today very nervous.

As you read further into the Book of Acts, it is quickly seen that the gift the Father promised is the outpouring of the Holy Spirit. As Jesus Himself said, "In a few days, you will be baptized with the Holy Spirit."

Our friend, Donnie Moore, had a wonderful way of putting it: "We Christians have a God who is Three in One...the Father, the Son, and What's His Name?" It is true that most people do not know much at all about the Holy Spirit. Throughout Church history, there have been great periods of time where this Third Person of the Trinity is put on the back shelf and almost forgotten.

Who is the Holy Spirit, and why did Jesus call the Holy Spirit a gift?

Years ago as my husband was reading through Acts, his attention was caught by the very first sentence and he pointed it out to me, "In my former book, Theophilus, I wrote about all that Jesus began to do and to teach until the day He was taken up to heaven, after giving instructions through the Holy Spirit to the apostles He had chosen" (Acts 1:1-2).

This is Luke speaking, the author of the Gospel of Luke and also the author of Acts. He was a traveling companion with the Apostle Paul and eyewitness to much of what happened in the early days of the Church.

Look what Luke says. "I wrote about all that Jesus began to do and teach." In other words, in the new book Luke is writing, he was telling Theophilus and the rest of us through the millenia what Jesus continued to do and teach through His Holy Spirit and His Church.

THERE IS MORE

Without the book of Acts, the flow of the Bible would be difficult to understand. How in the world do events go from the end of the Gospel accounts straight into the Epistles? Where did all of those churches come from? So much happened!

What occurred was that one hundred-twenty of Jesus' followers did wait for the gift the Father had promised, and as it says in Acts 2: 1-4: "When the day of Pentecost came, they were all together in one place. Suddenly a sound like the blowing of a violent wind came from heaven and filled the whole house where they were sitting. They saw what seemed to be tongues of fire that separated and came to rest on each of them. All of them were filled with the Holy Spirit and began to speak in other tongues as the Spirit enabled them."

That is Scripture, no less than Genesis 1:1: "In the beginning God created the heavens and the earth," or "John 3:16: "For God so loved the world that He gave His one and only Son, that whoever believes in Him shall not perish but have eternal life."

When Eli and I really began walking with God in college, we realized that we were in the middle of a group of Pentecostal Christians. I had very little reference for what this meant. I knew only that these people were awesome. They loved Jesus with all their hearts and they loved us, too. They were nice and encouraging, and they seemed much more concerned about our futures than we were. Both of us had been living like most everyone else on our campus, doing whatever we wanted without concern for God or anyone else.

We were living the typical college student life. But our new friends encouraged us to actually read the Bible and come to worship gatherings, and to think about what being a Christian really means and how that should impact our lives. They walked us through surrendering our wills to God, and trusting our lives to Him. And then they told us there was even more.

This "something more" is everywhere in Scripture and

throughout Church history once you start looking for it. It is more than receiving the Holy Spirit when you believe and confess that Jesus is Lord, which is truly the experience of every Christian (Titus 3:5-7.)

Jesus called this gift a "baptism" of the Holy Spirit, which is distinct from and subsequent to salvation; something more. More than the measure we are given at salvation which is an indwelling of the Holy Spirit, God offers a filling of His Spirit which is a baptism or immersion. Read the Chronicles of St. Francis of Assisi, the sermons and hymns of John and Charles Wesley, the works of Catherine Marshall—the list truly goes on and on, and crosses every generation and denominational line. Countless Christians have experienced this "something more."

I mentioned earlier that talking about this makes many people nervous. How do I know this? Because we have spent the last few decades ministering on a college campus! When we talk and teach about the Holy Spirit, it is not the pagan-background kids who get nervous. Actually, they tend to think that everything supernatural is very cool and fits perfectly with the king of the universe. No, it is the church kids who get nervous because somewhere along the way, some of them have been told it is wrong to look for something more today. This is an enormous theological discussion, and the arguments for and against are plentiful. For this little chapter, let it suffice to say that it is the dignity and honor of every man and woman who has access to a Bible to search the Scriptures and see for themselves.

The entire Bible is full of the Holy Spirit, starting in the very first few verses of Genesis. He was there and active from time without beginning, participating in the creation of all things, including the crown of creation, mankind. He is there when this age closes and a new eternal one begins, as we can read in the last few verses of Revelation 22, "The Spirit and bride say, 'Come!'"

All throughout the pages of Scripture, the Holy Spirit is

present and active, especially so after the great outpouring we can read about in Acts 2, the birthday of the Church. The Holy Spirit is none other than the Spirit of Jesus who plainly told His disciples in John 16:7-11:

> But very truly I tell you, it is for your good that I am going away. Unless I go away, the Advocate will not come to you; but if I go, I will send Him to you. When He comes, He will prove the world to be in the wrong about sin and righteousness and judgment: about sin, because people do not believe in Me; about righteousness, because I am going to the Father, where you can see Me no longer; and about judgment, because the prince of this world now stands condemned.

Once you start looking for the Spirit, it makes you really wonder how the Church can forget or ignore Him so frequently.

The Holy Spirit does many things. He creates, inspires, convinces, regenerates, comforts, intercedes and sanctifies*.

A huge piece of our faith is recognizing and rejoicing that Jesus left the glory of heaven and came to earth as Emmanuel, God With Us, in real time and in real flesh. In the time Jesus was actually here on earth, He was fully man and could only be in one place at a time. It must have been amazing for those early disciples to know Jesus face to face.

But now, in God's incredible way and in equally impactful measure, the Holy Spirit can be everywhere, all the time, in every age: God with each and every one of us. He does not just inspire or comfort one or two, but all of us, whether we live in Texas or Timbuktu.

A.W. Tozer said, "The Spirit-filled life is not a special, deluxe edition of Christianity. It is part and parcel of the total plan of God for His people." This gift is for any of us who will receive it. We can all walk with the Spirit of Christ and know Him just like our earliest brothers and sisters in the faith did.

How can we ignore the Holy Spirit or forget Him? I think if I were an evil enemy of God, a great strategy would be to render God's people weaker than they could be. I think I would try to blind them to every good thing God has provided. And this is just what the real enemy does. He tries to blind us to what God offers.

As we read further in Acts 1, the disciples are still confused as to why Jesus came and did all that He did. They have seen everything—His death, His glorious resurrection—and now the time has come for His ascension. Acts 1: 6-9 says:

> Then they gathered around him and asked him, "Lord, are You at this time going to restore the kingdom to Israel?" He said to them: "It is not for you to know the times or dates the Father has set by His own authority. But you will receive power when the Holy Spirit comes on you; and you will be My witnesses in Jerusalem, and in all Judea and Samaria, and to the ends of the earth." After He said this, He was taken up before their very eyes, and a cloud hid Him from their sight.

Here is the key, and this is why every Christian should seriously seek the "something more" of God. Jesus told His followers and He now tells us, "Wait for the gift My Father promised." Why? Jesus continued, "You will receive power when the Holy Spirit comes on you; and you will be My witnesses in Jerusalem, and in all Judea and Samaria, and to the ends of the earth."

Days later, the one hundred-twenty disciples who waited learned exactly what Jesus meant. They were baptized in the Holy Spirit and filled with power to be His witnesses. The same men and women who just weeks before had been afraid for their lives and in hiding, spilled out of that upper room and turned the whole world upside down with the good news of the kingdom of God. This gift of God removed the fear and doubt and self-centeredness of thinking that Jesus' kingdom was just for "me and mine," and gave them backbones of steel and a burning desire to tell everyone, everywhere, about Jesus and what He has done.

Two thousand years later, you and I are seeking Jesus because those first few waited and accepted this gift of the Father and, in His boldness and empowerment, shared their faith far and wide.

This gift of God is available to you, too. When we are born again, we have to learn to put down our sinful natures, and how to walk with God. All the things we have talked about are true and necessary. We must have discipline in our lives and we must be responsible for what we do. This is a big task. The whole world needs to hear of Jesus and His kingdom, and it is our job to tell them. But how kind the Lord is! He does not leave us alone or helpless in the effort.

More than my sister and her generous gifts, the Lord of heaven and earth sees each of us and knows exactly what we need, not just to live and make it, but to thrive. How sad it would be if we leave the packages my sister sends out on the doorstep. We would totally miss out on the treasures contained inside the box.

God takes delight in offering His great gift to each of us. This gift of His Holy Spirit that fills and empowers us is the very thing we need to thrive, live life to its fullness, and help many others know Christ.

Now it is up to you. Will you take the gift?

Application

Read the Book of Acts and pay close attention to every mention of the Holy Spirit. Especially note Acts 2, 8, 10 and 19, chapters which specifically feature people being baptized in the Holy Spirit. Be open and honest with the Lord as you study and seek.

From here I am going to leave the next steps purposefully unscripted. There is no set formula for receiving this gift. I have known people who asked once and received. Some were surrounded by people praying with them. Others were alone driving in their car, and even one person was in the shower. The experiences are as varied as the individuals.

* A helpful tool is a good study Bible. Mine is the Ryrie Study Bible, and this list is from the helps section in the back, under The Doctrine of the Holy Spirit. The Spirit is proved by His works: creating (Gen. 1:2), inspiring (2 Pet. 1:21), convincing men (John 16:8), regenerating (John 3:5-6), comforting (John 14:16), interceding (Rom. 8:26-27), and sanctifying (2 Thess. 2:13).

Books for Further Study:
Surprised by the Power of the Spirit by Jack Deere
Something More by Catherine Marshall

THIRTEEN

The Discipline of Waiting

It is so hard to wait! How humorous it is, then, that waiting seems to be what most of life requires: waiting for the semester to be over; waiting for that phone call; waiting in line, again; waiting for life to really begin. The happy bursts in life of beginnings and endings are sometimes drowned in the tedium of seemingly endless bouts of waiting.

The Bible is clear that this problem is not new or modern. Abraham and Sarah longed for a child, and everyone knows they had a little trouble waiting. Joseph waited for years in prison. David faced many long nights of waiting and wondering while Saul sought to kill him. The prophets and the whole nation of Israel longed and waited for the Messiah, their deliverer.

Waiting is nothing new. Waiting for direction from God in our lives, waiting for a spouse, waiting for a child, waiting for the weekend, for retirement, for whatever.

When the endless cycle of things we wait for is listed out this way, we face a compelling question: What is it, exactly, that we are waiting for? There is a real sense of, "This surely isn't all there is to life," or, "There must be something just ahead that will make everything right." We humans are hard-wired to have that feeling within us, to have a deep-within longing for things to be made right and perfect, for things to be the way they are supposed to be.

The season leading up to Christmas Day is called Advent, which means "the coming" (from Latin "to come"). The dictionary defines advent as the arrival of a notable person, thing or event. We celebrate, together with every follower of Christ all over the planet, the arrival of Jesus! Fully man yet fully God, the savior and redeemer of the world.

In Luke 2, we read that two precious, godly people had been waiting all their lives to see the Messiah. They had the Scriptures they had read and heard in the Temple, the promises of God to hold on to, yet they had not seen Him. Simeon had a revelation given by the Spirit. Still, he had not seen, but he believed and waited and watched.

Then one day, he did see. After all those years of waiting and watching, and into the Temple court came a puzzled and exhausted looking young couple with their newborn baby.

Imagine how Simeon felt. There He was, the Messiah! Every promise kept, every hope fulfilled, every fear and doubt dashed.

Today, you and I find ourselves alive during another endless season of waiting. It seems so long since Jesus has been here, and we begin to wonder if He ever will return. Yet there is one major difference during this period of waiting: Jesus really did come the first time. Try as the secularists may to erase this fact, the entire world calendar divides among Before Christ and In the Year of Our Lord. Our faith is historically validated, and millions and millions of saints can testify to Jesus' reality.

How then should we wait?

We can wait with confidence

"Do not let your hearts be troubled. You believe in God;

THE DISCIPLINE OF WAITING

believe also in Me. My Father's house has many rooms; if that were not so, would I have told you that I am going there to prepare a place for you? And if I go and prepare a place for you, I will come back and take you to be with Me that you also may be where I am. You know the way to the place where I am going." John 14: 1-4

Jesus is coming back; not if, but when. We don't have to wonder or be afraid that He has forgotten or changed His mind. Matthew 24:14 says, "And this gospel of the kingdom will be preached in the whole world as a testimony to all nations, and then the end will come." As soon as the gospel has been preached to every people group, Jesus will return.

Part of this is waiting in confidence is waiting with contentment. We can trust that, as we walk with Him in obedience, we are right where the Lord wants us. This is His plan and He is using us to build His kingdom.

We can wait with purpose

For the grace of God has appeared that offers salvation to all people. It teaches us to say "No" to ungodliness and worldly passions, and to live self-controlled, upright and godly lives in this present age, while we wait for the blessed hope—the appearing of the glory of our great God and Savior, Jesus Christ, who gave Himself for us to redeem us from all wickedness and to purify for Himself a people that are His very own, eager to do what is good. Titus 2: 11-14

Even though the world is constantly blaring its false version of what life is about, we know it is really about Jesus. Everything else is just fluff. Nothing compares to helping people know Jesus and making Him known.

Our waiting is not passive, but active. We take seriously the work of sharing the good news to the ends of the earth, and of making disciples of all nations (Matt. 28:18-20).

We can wait with eagerness

"But our citizenship is in heaven. And we eagerly await a Savior from there, the Lord Jesus Christ, who, by the power that enables Him to bring everything under His control, will transform our lowly bodies so that they will be like His glorious body" (Phil. 3: 20-21).

Just as every student counts down the days to the end of the semester, or as a bride and groom mark off every day on the calendar leading up to their wedding, we can eagerly look and point others to look for His coming. Keeping our eyes scanning for His coming holds everything here in its proper perspective. He is in control. World events and politics do not make God anxious. Jesus will return in the fullness of time.

Application

Read the Christmas passage of Luke 2 to your family when you gather for the holiday, and share the love of God with them. Take the opportunity to make a new tradition in your home by bringing the hopeful waiting of Advent into your family's routine.

Wait for the return of Jesus with confidence, purpose and eagerness. Keep on growing in the grace and knowledge of God, and continue to apply discipline into your life. I rejoice with you as you bear the good fruit of a life restored to order in mind, body and spirit.

FOURTEEN

Changed

Today is actually my birthday, and I am now forty-seven years old. Thirty years ago, I was a high school senior, finishing up that last semester and preparing to start a new chapter of life in college. I had no idea the wonderful journey that God was taking me on, or how radically my life and viewpoint were going to shift over the months after I arrived at the university.

It has been the blessing and honor of my life to be able to serve Jesus alongside my husband all these years on a college campus. The lessons in this book are things we have learned firsthand as we have walked with Jesus ourselves. We have been refined as we have been privileged to help many students.

This has proven to be a special place; many hundreds of people who were a part of this group are now in ministry and missions positions all over the world, and many thousands more are serving Jesus faithfully in the marketplace. Thirty years of data are in: Practicing spiritual disciplines helps us walk with God for the long-haul and helps us be transformed into the image of Jesus. I can tell you story after story about people I first met when they were eighteen years old and rather selfish, who are now some of the most godly people serving Jesus faithfully and fruitfully in some of the most challenging situations you can imagine.

Many young men came here angry and broken after being abandoned at a young age by their fathers. A student befriended them and brought them into the fellowship, and their hearts were changed by the love of God. They were set free from years of bitterness and hatred, and learned to apply the same things we have covered in this book. They learned how to have a real devotional life, real brothers and real responsibility, and began to be transformed day by day.

Now so many of them are the best husbands and fathers any family could ask for. Their own children will never know the sting and devastation of abandonment; only the care of a loving father.

I can think of face after face of young men and women who struggled with life-gripping substance or pornography abuse, and who were set free by the power of God. They learned to make drastic choices and changes in their lives, choosing to fill their minds, bodies and spirits with only healthy things. So many learned to walk in solid new habits of temperance and self-control, and have never looked back at their old lives. Their families are healthy and free from the chaos such addictions bring into a home.

More people than you would believe have overcome the shame and confusion resulting from sexual abuse in their childhoods. Jesus set them free and healed their hearts, and these young people learned to walk in health, with their sexuality surrendered to God. Hundreds of men and women who were harmed by abuse that should never happen to any child are now married with children of their own. The terrible cycle of abuse has been broken and their children will grow up safe from harm.

Angry people have become kind and hopeful; selfish people have become generous and giving; destructive people have become full of life and encouragement. People who never gave a thought for anyone other than themselves are now living lives of service that help others all over the world also know the great love of God. Knowing Jesus and surrendering our hearts and wills to Him changes everything, and walking in discipline with Him helps us become more like Him every day.

Sadly, I have also seen many people come close and then walk away. They came right up to the line, but for whatever reason did not want to trust God enough to cross over and really walk with Him. I hope that one day they have another opportunity to meet God and know Him.

There is no distinction in the sight of God between these two kinds of people—God made them all and deeply loves each one. It is not that some people are more favored and special to Him, and therefore have an easier time of walking with God their whole lives. No, each of us has a choice. We are responsible for the life and time we are given. God has done His great work, and His free gift of salvation is available to each of us.

Now it is up to us: His hand is extended. Will we choose to walk with Him into the abundant life He created us to live?

I pray this book has been an encouragement and blessing to you, no matter whether you are just meeting Jesus or have been walking with Him for many years. I hope you have been challenged to learn and grow in spiritual discipline, and to keep learning and growing all your days. You were created by God for this very time and place, and people around can be greatly impacted by your walk with Him. There are people you can reach and disciple who might be the very ones to open a heart, city or nation that previously was closed off to God.

Let the great love of God fill you and shape you and change you. Let everything He is doing in your heart and life spill out and impact your family, your friends and your neighbors. No matter what your starting point, I encourage you to start seeking the Lord with all your strength. Let the word of God wash your mind and the hope of God encourage your heart. In every way, may the Lord bless you and keep you, all the days of your life.

Application

A Prayer of Commitment:

Lord Jesus, I give my life to You; my hopes, dreams, talents, gifts, struggles, frustrations; all of it. I pray You help me live my life with You and for You. Help me to put You at the center of my life, and let everything else revolve around You. I ask that You help me live my life in such a way that I maintain the order of spirit, mind and body You are restoring in me, and my life would always shine steadily with Your hope and love, so others may know You. In Jesus' name and for His glory, amen.

References

The author acknowledges the contributions of these authors and publications.

Chapter 1
The definition of discipline as "restoring order to disorder in the mind, heart and spirit" is from Harvey Herman, Jr., *Discipleship by Design*, p. 61, published by Chi Alpha, 1991.

Chapter 2
The definition for love as "unselfishly choosing for the highest good of God and His Kingdom" is from Winkie Pratney, *A Handbook for Followers of Jesus,* pp. 28-29, published by Bethany Fellowship, Inc., 1977.

Chapters 3 & 4
The definitions for motive in the application exercise of chapter 3 and for obedience in the disobedience/rebellion section of chapter 4 are from Agapeforce, circa 1970. These definitions were a part of the script a troupe of clowns called Gingerbrook Fare used in kids' programs to teach big concepts to young people.

Chapter 8
Aspen trees, see "Quaking Aspen" on the U.S. Forestry Service website: fs.fed.us.

Chapter 11

Page 93, #7, "Love and laughter plow hard hearts," from Winkie Pratney in 21CR (a series on video). See www.winkiepratney.net/product/21-cr.

Intrinsic value is from Winkie Pratney, *The Nature and Character of God*, pp. 116-118, Bethany House Publishers, Minneapolis, 1988.